DEVELOPING HIGH IMPACT TEACHING

This vital book delves into key teaching strategies that drive student progress and enhance classroom learning. Both accessible and practical, it demonstrates how building routines and structures allows teachers to have a lasting positive impact on student's learning and offers the tools to ensure students feel supported and engaged throughout their learning journey.

Working as a practical guide for teachers at all stages, these chapters delve into topics such as delivering clear instructions, fostering metacognitive skills, assessing progress effectively, and leading impactful learning. *Developing High Impact Teaching* offers valuable advice on how to develop your students as active learners and participants in their own education, how to set up impactful routines and good learning habits, how to give clear instructions so students understand what success looks like, and how to use cognitive acceleration techniques to improve learning. It is an essential resource for any busy classroom teacher or school.

Designed with newly qualified teachers and those looking to refine their approach in mind, it emphasises evidence-based techniques rooted in Visible Learning principles. Through actionable advice and relatable insights, this book serves as an invaluable resource for educators seeking continuous growth and classroom success.

Cat Chowdhary is currently a Deputy Head of Teaching and Learning, living in Abu Dhabi with her family. With over a decade in education, she has developed a passion for pedagogy and shares practical insights into teaching best practices through her books, focusing on evidence-based research.

DEVELOPING HIGH IMPACT TEACHING

An Evidence-Based Guide

Cat Chowdhary

LONDON AND NEW YORK

Designed cover image: © Getty Images

First published 2025
by Routledge
4 Park Square, Milton Park, Abingdon, Oxon OX14 4RN

and by Routledge
605 Third Avenue, New York, NY 10158

Routledge is an imprint of the Taylor & Francis Group, an informa business

© 2025 Cat Chowdhary

The right of Cat Chowdhary to be identified as author of this work has been asserted in accordance with sections 77 and 78 of the Copyright, Designs and Patents Act 1988.

All rights reserved. No part of this book may be reprinted or reproduced or utilised in any form or by any electronic, mechanical, or other means, now known or hereafter invented, including photocopying and recording, or in any information storage or retrieval system, without permission in writing from the publishers.

Trademark notice: Product or corporate names may be trademarks or registered trademarks, and are used only for identification and explanation without intent to infringe.

British Library Cataloguing-in-Publication Data
A catalogue record for this book is available from the British Library

ISBN: 978-1-032-77267-7 (hbk)
ISBN: 978-1-032-77265-3 (pbk)
ISBN: 978-1-003-48212-3 (ebk)

DOI: 10.4324/9781003482123

Typeset in Interstate
by KnowledgeWorks Global Ltd.

CONTENTS

Acknowledgements vi
About the author vii

1. **Let's make learning visible - An introduction**   1
2. **High expectations and routines**   14
3. **Be clear and know your purpose**   40
4. **Leading the learning**   58
5. **Knowing where to go next**   80
6. **Metacognition in the classroom - Accelerating progress through effective task design**   95
7. **Progress in lessons - Know thy impact**   112

Index   129

ACKNOWLEDGEMENTS

Who would have thought I would write a book, let alone two? I want to say a big thank you to everyone who supported me when *So ... What Does an Outstanding Teacher Do* first came out. The lovely posts shared with me by so many teachers around the world, who read it and found it helpful, drove me to do it all again a second time round. Thank you for sharing your kind words.

I must remember to give a shout-out to my mum this time around – this book is for you, Chris! Thank you for giving me the tools to be where I am today.

And thank you to Shakeel – my wonderful husband. Sorry for the countless weekends I spent tucked away while you took over, keeping our three musketeers alive.

ABOUT THE AUTHOR

Cat Chowdhary is an experienced educator with over a decade of classroom expertise and a commitment to high-quality teaching and learning. As the Deputy Head of Teaching and Learning in a Charter School in Abu Dhabi, Cat brings a wealth of knowledge in curriculum development, instructional coaching, and behaviour management, working in both Primary and Secondary education. Previously, Cat served as the Head of English and Media Studies, before writing her first book, *So...What Does an Outstanding Teacher Do?*, focusing on providing practical strategies for impactful teaching. Her work is deeply informed by the Visible Learning values, ensuring an evidence-based approach to fostering student growth and teacher development.

ABOUT THE AUTHOR

1 Let's make learning visible - An introduction

That was a really good lesson, you had a good pace and clear objectives, however I didn't see any evidence of differentiation, teacher instruction, student-led activities, pair work, individual work, questioning, assessment for learning, high order thinking, use of technology....

And the list goes on! No wonder teachers feel so overwhelmed and stressed when they are being observed, what type of person can honestly complete all these approaches in one lesson? Who ever thought this was a realistic expectation? I mentioned in my previous book *So…What Does an Outstanding Teacher Do?* that the term 'outstanding' has increasingly become an elusive concept for teachers – no one really knows exactly what that looks like. Do 'outstanding' teachers really do all that? Of course not. All we have created is a trigger for teachers whenever they hear these unnecessary terms. Being 'outstanding' or 'effective' or even a 'good' teacher is never about what you 'pull off' in a one-off observation, but who you are on a daily basis.

As I write this, I am also creating a new lesson observation rubric for my teachers. It does bother me that I still must put a grading title where I live (outside the UK), when I know that will be all the teacher focuses on – 'Am I Outstanding?' I know that they will still get that gut-wrenching stomach tug that I used to get when I would hear the words 'well done, that was a good lesson with SOME outstanding features'. And just like a student receiving a grade with their feedback, anything after those words was lost on me. I would feel the blood rising to my face and be frantically looking at the clock to see when I could get out of that stuffy office so I could break down in my disappointment. I didn't listen to any of the constructive feedback being given after; I was too busy worrying if my observer could tell my ears were on fire, or worried my voice might wobble if she asked me a question. As a very anxious person, I know how stressful these situations are. I am so glad that Osted decided to get rid of lesson grading and moved their focus to impact.

However, that doesn't mean having a clear understanding of how you can improve isn't necessary. Just like with our students, it is important to have a success criteria so that you can continue to develop. I am not saying that if you do this, this, and this, you will be 'Outstanding' – that is not what any of this is about. What I am saying is, every teacher can always be better. It doesn't matter where on your teaching journey you are, there is always

DOI: 10.4324/9781003482123-1

room for improvement. As I have mentioned before, there is no such thing as the 'teaching plateau' – that myth was debunked years ago. The best place to start is with your mindset – think of Carol Dweck's (2017) 'power of yet' and know that building your self-efficacy will help you grow your confidence and make you better.

While my last book helped to (hopefully) distil the idea that 'outstanding' is something you can just pull off based on a tick list approach, what I wanted to focus on now is taking those concepts and applying them to the day-to-day lesson planning. Last time, I focused on mindsets and making small tweaks to learning in order to have a more significant impact, based on the research by John Hattie, exploring approaches to learning such as Piagetian programmes, metacognition, feedback, and building self-efficacy, which is all fantastic in theory – but what does that actually look like in a classroom? How do we plan our lessons so that we have a bigger impact? What I am noticing is teachers are still trying to cover EVERY teaching style into one lesson, leading to nothing actually getting done. Teacher retention in the UK alone is at an all-time low, with teachers exhausted and overwhelmed with their workload, which makes me question, why are the learners not doing more? We have fallen into this trap that we believe 'Me Teacher, Me Expert' (in your best caveman voice). Just because I am the teacher does not mean I have to do all the work. In fact, I shouldn't have to do it all, because I am building the skills in my learners to do it for themselves. Yes, learners need your knowledge, but they could just as easily get that knowledge from Google. What they need is to be taught how to think for themselves, how to go away and research, and how to be independent and resourceful. This spoon-feeding culture is giving them a disadvantage in life.

So, the question isn't 'how do I become an "outstanding" teacher?' Instead, the question is 'how do I have an impact in my lessons?' If you are having an impact, if your learners are making progress, then it doesn't matter what term you want to give yourself – you're doing an amazing job. For want of a better term, an 'outstanding' teacher knows their impact and utilises it in everything they are doing!

Let's make learning visible

It goes without saying ... teachers are busy people! We have marking, lesson planning, report writing, meetings, and actual teaching to do. So, it is not a surprise many teachers don't want to do anything else. It is hard enough as it is, let alone when someone comes in and revamps everything and introduces a new fad that is only going to last a year before everything gets changed and adapted again. I get it, many have lost faith in the system. But I honestly think we have been doing it all wrong for too long. We have this ingrained concept that we must work every hour we have, that we must work all evening and all weekend to make sure our learners succeed. Have we created a rod for our own backs? Why has this become an expectation for so many? But I assure you, there is a way to 'lighten the load'. What if I told you I very rarely take work home with me? What if I told you I almost never do work on a weekend? Shocking hey. How on earth could I possibly still get 'outstanding' results for my students and not have to slog through hours of overtime? I am a mum of three who are 8, 5, and 2 years old. I have learnt that for me to be good at both my jobs (work and mum), then I must work SMART. I often get asked 'how do you have time to be a teacher, a mum and write a book?' – I can assure you; I am not a Superwoman! Instead, I have developed a growth mindset, and I have used research and evidence to adapt the way I was doing things before – plus my final straw was when I brought my year 10 books home to mark and had to return them with some beautiful crayon decorations added. Mixing Mummy's work with child-care duties was not the best idea.

My improvements came about when I was introduced to Visible Learning (VL). VL is the life work of John Hattie, a professor at the Graduate School of Education in Melbourne, Australia. Why am I telling you this? Because he and his research have totally transformed education since his first book was published in 2008. Often considered the 'teaching's Holy Grail' (Mansell, 2008), this book provided teachers with thousands of meta-analysis research into what had (and didn't have) a significant impact on student progress. Over the years, there have been many more books, more extensive research, and even some revisions. His work has been praised by so many educational researchers, and some of these can be seen in the first few pages of his newest book, *Visible Learning: The Sequel* (2023), in which former headteacher Huw Thomas states 'Hattie's work enables us to see the effects of what teachers do in the classroom … In teaching we are often looking for those light-bulb moments of illumination. Hattie has mapped the hidden wiring'. I had that light-bulb moment the first time I was introduced to VL 7 years ago. I was sitting at the start of a new academic year, in a new school, in a new country. Half expecting the Senior Leadership Team (SLT) to stand up and conduct their usual spiel about their visions and their expectations, waiting for the groans of staff as they were told yet another thing would be changing or more paperwork would be added to their workload. Instead, I was very pleasantly surprised. We were introduced to impact cycles, effect sizes, and the key phrase 'know thy impact'. Who knew three small words would change my teaching career so drastically. Going from being someone who had almost believed in the teaching plateau myth, and almost accepting that perhaps I would always be just a 'good, with outstanding features' sort of teacher, my vision and outlook completely changed. Seriously – light-bulb moment!

Visible learning

For those of you who have not read my previous book *So…What Does An Outstanding Teacher Do* (Chowdhary, 2023), I'll just break down VL and effect sizes for you. John Hattie conducted some of the largest research into the influences on the learner's achievement, with a keen interest in finding out what could potentially affect academic performance, both positively and negatively. Using an effect size calculator (Figure 1.1), he was able to see where on the scale each influence was.

$$\text{Effect size} = \frac{\text{Mean}_{\text{treatment}} - \text{Mean}_{\text{control}}}{\text{Standard deviation}}$$

$$\text{Effect size} = \frac{\text{Mean}_{\text{after treatment}} - \text{Mean}_{\text{before treatment}}}{\text{Standard deviation}}$$

Figure 1.1 Effect size calculation

4 *Developing High Impact Teaching*

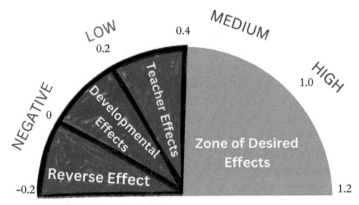

Figure 1.2 Barometer of influence
Adapted from Hattie (2012).

Using a 'barometer of influence' (Hattie, 2012), Hattie could range his influence from the negative -0.2 through to a positive +1. Anything above 0 would indicate a positive influence, with 0.40 being the hinge-point, meaning anything above this was in the zone of desired effects (Figure 1.2).

The main premise of VL is the encouragement of making learning more apparent and observable. It is not just about teaching learners' subject-specific concepts, not just what they are supposed to know, but also teaching them how to learn, and how to evaluate their own learning. Through research and evidence, VL provides more effective approaches to teaching and learning to ensure progress is made by all, in a one-size-fits-one method. Instead of doing things because 'I have always done it this way', VL encourages educators to assess their own impact in the classroom, improving and refining their practice to maximise their potential. With data in abundance in schools, it's so important that teachers start observing and analysing their data so that they can adapt their teaching to the individual needs of their learners. By making learning more personalised through differentiated instruction, you can keep learners motivated and improve their performance.

By looking through Hattie's research, you can see to what extent different elements can impact learner progress. Some examples of some of the effect sizes taken from Hattie's new book (2023) are given in Table 1.1 to give you an idea.

Table 1.1 Example of effect sizes

Illness	−0.44	Negative impact
Boredom	−0.33	Negative impact
Reducing class sizes	0.17	Small positive impact
Self-regulation strategies	0.21	Potential to accelerate
Clear success criteria	0.42	Potential to accelerate
Classroom management	0.43	Positive impact
Feedback	0.58	Potential to accelerate
Collective teacher efficacy	1.34	Considerable acceleration

Source: Adapted from Hattie, J. 2023

It makes sense that there will be elements of a child's life that would have a negative impact on their learning. It goes without saying, a child suffering from abuse at home is going to have serious consequences on a child's ability to learn. Boredom also has a negative impact on a learner's progress. One of the toughest parts of being a teacher (especially a secondary teacher) is trying to keep students motivated. This is where we must work miracles and become psychologists, carers, and comedians all in one. Very hard to do when you know you often have some tiresome part of the curriculum you have to get through to prepare them for an exam or assessment. Reeves et al. (2023) noted that most students do come to class full of motivation, just unfortunately, they are not always consistent with the teacher's expectations. This will often lead to those common discussions in the staff room, 'I just can't motivate them', 'They are just not interested', and 'I can't get through to them'. But you must remember, most motivations are driving through an idea of striving towards a goal, mastering what they are doing. If the learners can't see the goal in front of them, then motivation will often decrease. As Hattie (2023) points out, boredom is 'the antithesis of high self-efficacy' (p. 106) and indicates that it often suffers because the work being set lacks any value or meaning. This is the first step to making learning visible – what is the bigger picture? Why are they doing this? What do they gain from it? Increase their confidence by making the work engaging, share a success criteria with them so they can see where they are and where they need to go, and give them a goal to strive for.

While boredom can have a significant negative impact, as we can see, goal setting can accelerate learner progress, so it goes without saying how important it is to introduce one to minimise the other. Start the year by knowing your class, their data, and their strengths and weaknesses – give them a realistic goal and push them towards it. Regularly reflect on this goal with your learners and once it has been met, move that goal post a little more. As you watch your learners' self-efficacy grow, as they begin to grow confidence through mastery, their motivation will skyrocket. Their success is limitless.

Now, I have had many conversations and debates with teachers from all around the world regarding effect sizes, the age-old 'I have done it this way for years and it has never been a problem for me'. Many will say they disagree with some of these effect sizes, most significantly the idea that reduced class sizes only have a low positive impact. And I get it – sometimes there is a lot more to it than just a number on a spreadsheet. A teacher is going to be able to get more done with a smaller class of 15 than with a class of 30. A class of 30 top set high achievers is a lot easier to teach than a bottom set class of 30 boys. Hattie often talks about how research is not necessarily data and facts, but instead an interpretation – the story. The problem with this, though, is everyone can see the same research in completely different ways. Along the way, there have been many misconceptions about research, especially Hattie's effect sizes. When we look at Hattie's effect sizes, we have to look at the bigger picture and not as stand-alone grading. In an interview with Sarah Montague for BBC Radio 4 (2014), Hattie discussed the controversial effect sizes for class sizes and stated that what really matters isn't how many learners are in the class, but that the teacher is adapting and learning to be an expert in their class, no matter what the size is. It is again about reflecting on a regular basis and making our teaching visible. If we spent as much time trying to upskill ourselves at being better, as we do, moaning that we can't do our jobs properly because there are too many in the classroom, we'd all be outstanding. It is easier for us to dismiss data and research because it doesn't fit our narrative than it is to actually do something about it. And this isn't a moan at teachers – I know, I've been there with a class of 30 year 8 students (predominantly boys) who, because of COVID, hadn't had proper routines and schooling for 3 years; they initially made me feel like an NQT again. I was the first to say 'HELP'! I know it is easier said than done when you're in the thick of it. But when you do stop and re-evaluate, and look at your class in a reflective way, I assure you, you will have a better outcome. I'm not saying it's going to transform overnight, but just like any habit or routine you are trying to change, you have to be consistent and give yourself time to embed before you start noticing the significant improvements – and that is when your life gets a lot easier. Hattie concludes in his interview that your learners' academic growth ultimately comes down to teacher expertise. The decisions you make on a daily basis are the most important thing for school success. When you are strong and confident, your learners are strong and confident, and your school is strong and confident. I know many will say 'easier said than done' – and you're not wrong; it's not easy changing the way you teach, the style you've had for 10, 15, or 20 years. But it is necessary if you want to make those changes and make your teaching and learning more visible. We can all continue down the 'but this just works for me' route, and that's fine, but just think what you could achieve if you developed a growth mindset.

The important thing to remember when looking into research is that it is so important to read and evaluate it (Wolfe & Brandt, 1998). For every piece of evidence you come across, you will find those who criticise and try to disprove it. One opponent of Hattie is researcher, Robert Slavin, who argued that 'The essential problem with Hattie's meta-analyses is that they accept the results of the underlying meta-analyses without question' (2018). However, Hattie has always stuck to the point that teachers and SLT should not just focus on influences with the highest effects. It is not about 'let's only do the high end and stop doing those with lower effect sizes'. As a teacher, you just need to be aware of the impact, gather the evidence, and find the strategies that work best for you. In 2018 Hattie addressed some more of these criticisms in his blog post *Clearing the Lens: Addressing the Criticisms of the Visible Learning Research* (Table 1.2).

So, you may have your questions regarding the research, and as I mentioned before, it is good to question it. I am just telling you from my perspective what has worked for me. VL is about getting teachers to reflect on their own practice using the research in front of them. By collecting this information and learning more about it, we begin to understand what will help drive our learners forward. Through adapting our practices, we can start preparing our learners to be able to function in the complex work of adulthood.

In order for me to break this down further, my chapters are going to indicate the flow of a lesson. Think of this book as a gigantic lesson plan, thinking about each step of planning and providing you with research and examples that can help you have more of an impact at each stage. To give you some more insight, here is a little breakdown of each chapter for you. While I suggest you read them chronologically, you may want to focus on one chapter specifically, so you can see here what I will be covering and head straight over there if you need to.

Table 1.2 Hattie's criticisms

Criticism	Hattie's Response
1. You keep on adding more meta-analysis and more influences	The nature of research is to continue to question and validate studies, so more will naturally be added over time. Should anything change, Hattie wants to be the first to acknowledge this, but so far, every new addition has just continued to confirm the VL model
2. VL research includes old studies	It is important to keep historical findings in mind. Knowing what has occurred in the past will help inform research moving forward. It allows us to ensure old, disproved opinions do not rise again, while also understanding what worked best before and developing this further in the future
3. It is wrong to only focus on influences that have the highest effect sizes and ignore the lowest ones	Hattie agrees with this! Effect sizes are a summary, not a hierarchy. Just because an effect size is not in the 'desired zone' does not mean it isn't worthwhile – instead, it just needs more research and exploration. An example given is homework in primary schools as a 0-effect size. It does not mean that homework should not be given, but more focus needs to be put into improving the effects of homework. With more research and a better understanding of what type and in what way it should be given means that in the future the effect size of this could change
4. Research excludes qualitative studies that might support some lower ranked influences	You cannot quantify qualitative data, so no, they weren't initially used. However, there have been developments since the first VL book was published, where more qualitative studies have taken place
5. VL ignores the debate about content or what subject matter is worth learning	VL has never been about what is and isn't worth learning. The purpose of VL is to understand what works best in developing learner achievement
6. VL only focuses on achievement, but schools are about much more than that	In the first VL book, Hattie made a clear comment that there are many outcomes of schooling; however, that book was only focusing on learner achievement. However, since then there has been much more focus on motivation, interest, and affect as well as 'How We learn' (Hattie & Donoghue, 2016). As the research develops, so the other areas of schooling get covered

Chapter 2: High expectations and routines

In this chapter I will focus on the importance of establishing and maintaining routines and high expectations in the classroom. Behaviour management is fundamentally the foundation of effective teaching and learning – let's get this right, right from the start of the school year!

I know there are so many challenges facing teachers today, particularly concerning behaviour in the classroom. Many teachers struggle with maintaining order and will often agree that this is usually the driving force behind why teaching and learning is limited. We have all experienced those disruptive classes – the ones where you feel like you're in some sort of comedy movie. 'Ben, stop punching Michael!', 'David, this is not the time or place to start decorating your shoes with Tipp-Ex!', and 'No Lucy, I am not going to tell you about my plans for dinner right now!' Until we can get these disruptive behaviours squashed, we can't teach a term of Shakespeare's Romeo and Juliet!

I will focus mainly on the works of Tom Bennett's *Running the Room* (2020) and his suggestions on how to reinforce routines in the classroom. Bennet argues that routines are the building blocks of our classroom culture and should be clear, modelled, and repeated until they become second nature to learners. The importance of these routines lies in your ability to create a structured environment where they know what is expected of them, therefore reducing those disruptive behaviours and fostering a learning atmosphere focused on success.

Another key element of enforcing better behaviour in the classroom is through positive reinforcement. Simple things like greeting your learners at the door with a smile and a hello can help to slowly shift those behaviour patterns and encourage engagement in the lesson. Some strategies I explore in this chapter are from the research of Paul Dix, in his book *When the Adults Change, Everything Changes: Seismic Shifts in School Behaviour* (2020). Dix advocates for the use of countdowns to regain your learner's attention, setting clear instructions using the TROGS technique (Time, Resources, Outcomes, Groupings, and Stop signals), and reflective questioning to check for understanding and promote self-reflection among learners. These strategies help maintain order and focus, allowing teachers to deliver instructions more effectively and learners to engage more productively.

Moreover, the chapter emphasises the importance of consistency in routines across the school. When all teachers in a school adopt similar routines and expectations, it helps learners understand and meet behavioural standards more easily, reducing confusion and promoting a more orderly school environment.

Chapter 3: Be clear and know your purpose

Once clear routines and behaviour management strategies are embedded into our lesson, we can then begin to concentrate on the learning itself. This chapter focuses on the importance of teacher clarity; with an effect size of 0.84, it is imperative that we concentrate on what our expectations are and how we get this across to our learners. When your teaching is organised and forthright, your learners are clear on what the expectations are, allowing them to work more effectively with a stronger sense of their own progress. The decisions you make in the classroom can have a significant impact on achievement (Danielson, 2002).

This chapter investigates ways of making sure our expectations are clear and easily understood by our learners, with a specific focus on backwards planning. When you know the outcome of your lesson, you can see a clearer pathway and start planning activities that are going to lead to success. A great way to do this is to identify your desired learning results, determine what you will consider acceptable evidence, and plan your learning experiences and instructions to achieve your desired outcome. By starting with your end goal and planning backwards, you ensure that your instructional steps lead to your desired learning outcomes. Not only this means you are planning more coherent and focused lessons, but this method also helps align your objectives with the actual tasks and success criteria your learners need to meet, therefore minimising any confusion and maximising your instructional effectiveness.

Let's make learning visible   9

This chapter will delve into some practical strategies for giving clear instructions, sharing some ideas from Micheal Feely and Karlin (2023), such as the 'Say It to See It' technique, which emphasises positive reinforcements and clear, precise directives. When using this technique, you begin to praise your learners who are following your instructions correctly, describing those desired behaviours instead of fixating on the negatives. When learners understand the purpose behind the tasks, they tend to be more motivated to do them, again reinforcing the positive learning environments discussed in Chapter 2.

Assessment and the use of success criteria are also a key focus of this chapter and are pivotal elements of effective teaching. Using continuous formative assessment to monitor the progress of your learners and adjusting your teaching strategies accordingly are excellent examples of what an effective teacher does. It is so importance to set specific, and measurable success criteria that align with your lesson objectives, and using frameworks like Bloom's and SOLO Taxonomy can help you create clear learning objectives and success criteria that promote both surface-level and deep learning.

On top of all that, this chapter will also explore the importance of clarity in your instructional delivery. We don't want to overwhelm our learners, so we need to break down instructions into simple, sequential steps. When planning your lessons, reflect on what you already know about your learners – what are the potential pitfalls? What strategies are you going to prepare to address these? What are the key pieces of information that need to be shared and how can you break it down, so it is easily understood by all?

'Be Clear and Know Your Purpose' underscores that clear and purposeful lesson planning and instruction are fundamental to successful teaching. Using backwards planning, explicit clear objectives, clear instructions, and a strong success criteria so learners know how to be successful will create an effective learning environment that supports the learner's achievement. Continuous assessment and reflective practice further ensure that both you and your learners stay aligned with your educational goals, fostering a more engaging and productive learning experience for all.

Chapter 4: Leading the learning

This chapter explores the importance of minimising teacher talk and increasing student-led activities to foster self-regulation and problem-solving skills in your learners. It delves into the practical aspects of how teachers can encourage more learner engagement and reduce their own dominance in the classroom. We often see ourselves as performers, but we want to facilitate learning, not become the 'sage on the stage'. We have lots of roles to play in the classroom, but an effective teacher knows how to balance these roles to engage their learners. They know when to take the lead and when to step back and allow the learners to take charge of their learning.

One of our roles is to be able to measure learning in the classroom. We can often misinterpret signs of engagement, such as our learners 'listening' and completing work or answering questions. However, 'busy' learners are not necessarily indicators of progress. One of the many limitations to progress is excessive teacher talk – this is a major issue in the classroom, often stemming from the idea that we, the teachers, are the experts and should therefore impart as much knowledge as possible to our learners. But, as this chapter will show, extensive teacher talk often leads to overloading the working memory of our learners, leading to disengagement. Why are we doing all the work, when we know this is not impactful?

This chapter will explore Cognitive Load Theory and how the brain processes and stores information, outlining the following three types of cognitive load:

Intrinsic Cognitive Load: The inherent difficulty of the material.
Extraneous Cognitive Load: Distractions that interfere with learning.
Germane Cognitive Load: The mental effort required to create new schemas and understand new information.

We need to minimise the extraneous load and manage the intrinsic load to achieve better outcomes for our learners. To help with this, this chapter will explore effective strategies such as:

- **Chunking Information:** Breaking down information into smaller, manageable sections.
- **Retrieval Practice:** Regularly revisiting material to move it from short-term to long-term memory.
- **Interactive Lessons:** Engaging learners actively rather than having them passively listen.

As well as this, we must focus on the importance of our ultimate goal - to create dynamic learner-led opportunities. By minimising teacher talk and focusing on learner-led activities, we can better engage them, helping to develop essential skills for their future.

Chapter 5: Knowing where to go next

This chapter delves a little more specifically into the importance of a success criteria and how it can be used to significantly enhance learners' progress. It is so important that we integrate our success criteria, visibly into our lessons, to allow our learners to know where they are heading. Hattie highlights the impact of a success criteria and goal setting, through the significant effect sizes of 0.88 and 0.90, underscoring the importance of providing your learners with clear, achievable targets to foster motivation, engagement, and self-regulation.

The aim of this chapter is to provide you with a clear definition of what a success criteria is, how to create one, and how to then use it successfully in the classroom. Using Almarode et al.'s (2021) research, I focus on three key questions - 'What am I learning?', 'Why am I learning this?', and 'How will I know that I have learned it?' This approach enables learners to monitor their progress and make necessary adjustments. To help demonstrate the creation of a success criteria, I refer to the use of SOLO Taxonomy (structure of observed learning outcome) in order to show how it can be broken down into different levels, from basic understanding to advanced application and evaluation. Having differentiation in your success criteria helps meet the diverse needs of your learners, and can be done through tiered success criteria such as with SOLO, and also through flexible groupings, scaffolded support, visual aids, student choice, and the use of technology, as this will create an inclusive learning environment.

There is a strong emphasis on the importance of co-constructing your success criteria with your learners, to ensure they fully understand and internalise the learning objectives, creating a collaborative approach to reduce potential rigidity, while also promoting creativity and flexibility within a structured framework. However, like with everything we do in the classroom, there are challenges in creating and implementing success criteria, including issues of circular learning intentions, procedural focus, product-focus, measurability, and direction setting. To help combat these challenges, I have tried to provide some strategies that will enable success criteria to be more meaningful and supportive of deep learning.

Once the success criteria have been created and understood by all involved, there is also a need to continuously refer back to it throughout the learning process using it as a form of self-assessment, peer feedback, and ongoing progress monitoring. This approach helps learners develop their self-efficacy, reflective practices, and independence.

Chapter 6: Metacognition in the classroom – Accelerating progress through effective task design

In this chapter, I wanted to explore the concept of metacognition in education and how it can accelerate learning. When we talk about metacognition, what we are really dealing with is our ability to become aware of our thinking processes and how we best learn. When we better understand how we learn, we are able to apply those strategies to a range of different contexts, improving our outcomes. As we build our ability to use metacognitive regulation, we are able to plan how to approach tasks, monitor our performance, and then evaluate the effectiveness of the strategies we used.

This chapter focuses on the importance of metacognition in education in order to achieve better academic outcomes. The research tells us that using metacognitive prompts regularly in the classroom helps to foster our learner's ability to regulate their own processes, building their confidence and equipping them with the tools to become lifelong learners.

Some of the suggested strategies focus on teaching explicit instruction, where learners use specific techniques, such as setting SMART goals, through seeing their teacher modelling these strategies. Other strategies such as self-questioning before, during, and after tasks allow learners to monitor their understanding and performance.

This chapter will delve into the Gradual Release of Responsibility (GRR) model, in which we transfer responsibility of learning from us to our learners through the 'I do', 'We do', and 'You do' approaches, guiding them through tasks with support to eventually move them on to working independently and collaboratively without us. Just like learning to ride a bike.

Using metacognitive strategies has such a significant impact on our learning outcomes, and by incorporating these strategies into everyday classroom practices, we encourage a more reflective and self-directed learning environment. Our ultimate goal is to create lifelong learning, building the skill to be able to plan, monitor, and evaluate our learners.

Chapter 7: Progress in lessons – Know thy impact

For my final chapter, I wanted to finish with thinking about progress in lessons and knowing your impact in the classroom. While we can incorporate all these fantastic strategies into our lesson, at the end of the day, our goal is to ensure our learners are consistently moving forward. It is not enough to just cover curriculum content and push for high grades – we must focus on learner progress over time. In order to do this, we must regularly assess how our learners are building on prior knowledge and developing new skills to move from surface learning to deep learning.

This chapter will break down the three types of assessment – assessment for, of, and as learning. Each of these plays an important role in tracking progress, from assessing understanding within lessons, through formative quizzes and questioning, to encouraging reflection in order to set goals for improvement and empowering ownership of learning. But these are not just stand-alone concepts; they work in conjunction with each other.

When we are measuring progress, we must ensure every learner, no matter their starting point, is being appropriately challenged. This might mean scaffolding tasks for some learners while also providing more complex activities for our more able learners to stretch their thinking. Through feedback that is timely, specific, and actionable, we are able to help our learners understand where they are, where they are going, and how to get there.

Progress isn't a simple linear line; it isn't going to be straight from A to B. Real learning involves ups and downs and setbacks, but by incorporating some of the AfL and AaL strategies into your lessons, you can begin to ensure you are making a real difference in the learning journeys of all your learners.

Just as I said in my previous book (Chowdhary, 2023), this book is about being reflective of your teaching practices, looking at what you have 'always done' and evaluating if that is still working. As we work through a typical lesson plan, let's find some great ways to ensure the impact is taking place in your classes. And just like before, I hope, as you read through these chapters, you can do at least one of these three things:

- **Confirm** the knowledge you already have, validate what you are currently doing, and feel confident that you are doing a good job.
- **Learn** new ideas of how you could make small tweaks in your own classrooms with your students.
- **Share** the knowledge, research more, and keep up to date with new pedagogy.

References

Almarode, J., Fisher, D., Frey, N., & Thunder, K. (2021). *The success criteria playbook: A hands-on guide to making learning visible and measurable*. Corwin Press.

Bennett, T. (2020). *Running the room: The teacher's guide to behaviour*. John Catt Educational Ltd.

Chowdhary, C. (2023). *So...what does an Outstanding teacher do: A visible learning evidence based approach*. Routledge.

Danielson, L. (2002). Developing and retaining quality classroom teachers through mentoring. *The Clearing House: A Journal of Educational Strategies, Issues and Ideas*, 75(4), 183-185. https://doi.org/10.1080/00098650209604927

Dix, P. (2020). *When the adults change, everything changes: Seismic shifts in school behaviour*. Independent Thinking Press.

Dweck, C. S. (2017). *Mindset: Changing the way you think to fulfil your potential*. Robinson.

Feely, M., & Karlin, B. (2023). *The teaching and learning playbook: Examples of excellence in teaching*. Routledge.

Hattie, J. (2012). *Visible learning for teachers: Maximizing impact on learning*. Routledge, Taylor & Francis Group.
Hattie, J. (2018, June 22). *Clearing the lens: Addressing the criticisms of the VISIBLE LEARNING research*. Corwin Connect. https://corwin-connect.com/2018/06/clearing-the-lens-addressing-the-criticisms-of-the-visible-learning-research/
Hattie, J. (2023). *Visible learning: The sequel*. Taylor & Francis Ltd.
Hattie, J., & Donoghue, G. (2016). *How we learn*. Routledge.
Mansell, W. (2008). Research reveals teaching's Holy Grail. *Tes Magazine*. https://www.tes.com/magazine/archive/research-reveals-teachings-holy-grail
Montague, S. (Host). (2014, August 20). John Hattie (No. 6) [Audio podcast episode]. In *The Educators*. BBC Radio 4. https://www.bbc.co.uk/sounds/play/b04dmxwl
Reeves, J., Ryan, R. M., Cheon, S. H., Matos, L., & Kaplan, H. (2023). *Supporting student motivation*. Taylor & Francis.
Slavin, R. (2018, June 21). John Hattie is wrong. *Robert Slavin's Blog*. https://robertslavinsblog.wordpress.com/2018/06/21/john-hattie-is-wrong/
Wolfe, P., & Brandt, R. (1998). What do we know from brain research? *ASCD Educational Leadership*, 56(3). https://www.ascd.org/el/articles/what-do-we-know-from-brain-research

2 High expectations and routines

This is all well and good but…

Often, one of the biggest roadblocks, when it comes to improving teaching and learning, is behaviour. We all know it is almost impossible to do fun, cool activities when the learners are not listening, and chaos has erupted. 'This is all well and good but…' is usually one of the first comments I hear when I am delivering professional development sessions, as many teachers struggle with the management of behaviour in class, limiting how much freedom they can actually give to their learners. I remember teaching one year 8 class, where, if I gave them a slight inch, they took the whole ten miles and ran with it. When I turned my back, there would be paper planes flung across the room, water bottles squirted at someone, pens snapped, display boards ripped, and phallic symbols drawn on tables and walls – it almost sounds like a Carry-On comedy show. When starting my career, I had to learn very quickly the importance of setting classroom routines and having high expectations – which is easier said than done when you are an ECT (early careers teacher). You're nervous, you're not quite sure yourself what your expectations are, and the learners sniff it out and smell the fear in you. We have all been there, but I promise you, there is light at the end of the tunnel. Often, we forget that our learners need to be taught how to behave. While we can often take manners for granted, many learners come from home backgrounds where the only attention they get is negative, they don't all have the support of parents teaching them right from wrong, and rarely get positive praise. I think back to my upbringing; I was fortunate to have parents that would correct my behaviour and model to me how to conduct myself in public. I'm not saying I was a saint growing up, far from it, but I was provided with the tools to learn vicariously through the adults in my life. I was one of the lucky ones. Imagine going home to an environment that is full of intimidation and aggression. Difficult behaviour is very hard to unlearn – but it is possible. Learners need role models – and as teachers, that becomes part of our job.

Will Fastiggi (2019) discusses the fundamental role behaviour management has in his article 'The Three Pillars of Successful Behaviour Management' where he argues that effective behaviour management strategies are the key to successful teaching and learning. Without developing these foundations first, behaviour can dampen the morale of teachers, limiting their creativity in the classroom. According to the Department of Education's 2018 report on teacher retention, 'teachers who were planning lessons afresh found it difficult to be creative

High expectations and routines   15

in their planning and teaching, due to being hindered by time or challenges around pupil behaviour' (p. 18). Many teachers reported that behaviour issues in class often make it challenging to maintain good lesson outcomes, leading to more work as they would then need to follow up with logging the issues and contacting home, as opposed to well-behaved lessons, where learning flourishes and learners are motivated and engaged. I think it is fair to say that often a bad lesson leaves a longer-lasting effect on us than good ones do. It is easy to spiral into that depth of despair when you feel like every day is a battle and you go home physically drained – I know many teachers who have the scars to prove it and the statistics tell us that 9.9% of teachers left the profession in 2022 (Schools Week, 2023), which is the highest rate since 2017/18; many put this down to poor behaviour in lessons.

So, what can we do to help solve this problem? While I can advise some strategies in the classroom, true behaviour improvement has to be a whole culture shift within schools. As much time and focus needs to be put into creating a truly sustainable behaviour policy and mindset, as there is in lesson planning and subject knowledge, which comes from the top down. As Paul Dix mentioned in his 2017 book *When the Adults Change*, the behaviour policy needs to be consistent to be effective and a collective response. It all starts with a mindset shift. John Hattie's (2023) newest evaluation of classroom management generated an effect size of 0.43 in his book *Visible Learning: The Sequel*, showing that a rise in learner achievement typically was seen in lessons that had created a positive environment, where there were clear learner-teacher relationships and fairness, and there was a further increase to learner attainment when able to diminish any potential disruptions to learning with an effect size of 0.82. Ofsted (2024) highlights the importance of 'having a calm and orderly environment in the school and the classroom, as this is essential for pupils to be able to learn'. I mentioned in my previous book the analogy of flies in a jar (Figure 2.1) – once they were captured in a jar

Figure 2.1 Flies in a jar

16 *Developing High Impact Teaching*

with the lid screwed on, at first the flies tried desperately to fly out of the top of the jar, but after countless hopeless attempts, eventually, they all stopped trying. Then one day the lid was removed, giving the flies freedom to leave, but due to their conditioning, the flies didn't even attempt to make their escape. They had been constantly reminded that they couldn't leave, so they never tried again. While I appreciate this story has many scientific flaws, the metaphor is clear – don't condition your learners to believe what society already thinks of them. It is so easy to dismiss a child because of his or her background. Those staff room conversations of 'oh, I don't even bother with *that* one anymore' or 'good luck with her!' are just what is wrong with mindsets towards behaviour in schools.

These negative views, while you think are just part of staffroom gossip, are actually the breeding ground for systemic negativity and prejudice. Paul Dix (2017) talks in depth about how, before we can even consider improving learner behaviour, we need to change the adults. If it is not being modelled from the top down, then you will constantly be fighting an uphill battle. These types of comments are also prime examples of people who have very fixed mindsets, allowing them to be defeated by what is being perceived as 'a lost cause'. Carol Dweck (2017) is the leading researcher behind the idea of growth and fixed mindsets (Figure 2.2). With fixed mindsets, people are less likely to change their attitudes towards challenges, fearing failure and easily giving up when things get hard. Whereas, by developing a growth mindset, you will find people striving to improve and develop. They tend to be more resilient in stressful times and seek ways of developing and improving the situations they find

The Power of a Growth Mindset

Growth Mindset
- Finds inspiration in others success.
- Perseveres in the face of failure.
- Accepts criticism and uses it to adapt.
- Embraces challenges.

Fixed Mindset
- Feels threatened by other people's success.
- Feedback is taken as a personal attack.
- Gives up at the first sign of failure.
- Doesn't like challenge.

@Pedagogy_Teacher

Figure 2.2 Growth mindset

themselves in. They look at the bigger picture and question rather than ignore. For example, rather than seeing a learner as a 'lost cause', they respond to the situation by looking for the root causes and finding solutions to help. When you surround yourself with others who equally have a fixed mindset and continue to be negative, this will encourage you to do the same. Whereas evidence shows that being around positivity helps support mental health, builds resilience, and promotes happiness and well-being (Whalen-Harris, 2023).

In the 1960s, Robert Rosenthal conducted an experiment into how higher expectations can lead to improved outcomes in an elementary school in California, referred to as the Pygmalion effect (Figure 2.3). During this experiment, he said, he tested the students' IQ and then put them into groups. Following the test, he gave the teachers a list of learners who, he said, were 'intellectual bloomers' and were destined to be high achievers, but he did not give the teachers the actual IQ scores. As a result of this, the teachers' expectations of those learners were much higher than the rest of the class, and as a result they outperformed the others. The truth was, they weren't necessarily high performers, and in fact it was just a mixture of abilities in the class – but the teachers put more time, effort, and focus into those they 'believed' were higher.

When you have a certain belief in others, that will impact how you behave around them and treat them. So, when you believe someone is better, stronger, and more able, then you will treat them as such. As a result of this, their self-efficacy grows, and they begin believing themselves to be of that calibre. This then leads to them behaving in accordance with that expectation – if you expect them to be hard workers, they will start being hard workers, which merely reinforces your initial opinion and so the cycle continues. As Rosenthal points out, 'When we expect certain behaviors of others, we are likely to act in ways that make the expected behavior more likely to occur' (Rosenthal & Babad, 1985).

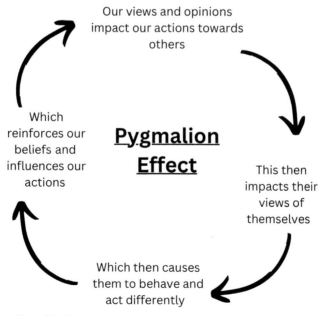

Figure 2.3 Pygmalion effect

18 *Developing High Impact Teaching*

Behaviour management can be a challenge; you are dealing with learners from a range of different backgrounds, learning to cope with their own emotions, and not knowing how to express themselves. From early years through to Sixth Form – you will come across a range of behaviours. In the face of dealing with children, behaviour management becomes a job in itself; you have to teach them how to behave. But through a consistent and collective approach, you can develop your emotional competence and organisation, to help create a calmer and more effective environment to provide learners with the opportunities to understand their emotions and build their self-efficacy. When you have low expectations of your learners, with a fixed mindset, then you begin to justify their behaviour; you give it an excuse and label them as 'unfixable' and they continue their lives like flies in the jar. As Paul Dix (2017) points out, children are desperate for us to offer them our hands and guide them, but often we adults get annoyed by their responses too quickly and remove our hands away too soon. Those children who keep pushing and testing the adults are usually the ones who need us the most. They are so used to people walking away; they test to see who will be left, even after all the 'bad' behaviour. When I am faced with a difficult situation in which a pupil is really testing my patience, I remind myself of the old fable of the Sun and the Wind (Figure 2.4). Once the Wind and the Sun were watching a young man walking in a field, and the Wind decided to make a bet with the Sun – 'I bet I can get the man's coat off'. The Sun agrees to this challenge and allows the Wind to begin. The Wind blew and blew so hard, but all the man did was wrap his coat tighter around him. Then, when it was the Sun's turn, all it did was shine brightly, and the young man simply removed his coat and basked in the sunshine. Where the Wind tried to use its power and force, the Sun simply used sunshine and warmth.

Figure 2.4 Sun and the Wind

High expectations and routines 19

As Paul Dix (2017) points out, we don't want to create a culture of fear, anxiety, and punishment, we want to grow with love.

Building strong relationships is so important when setting out your expectations with learners. Our goal is to have a positive impact on our learners, and by building those teacher-learner relationships, it allows us to have a strong effect on their lives (Hattie & Yates, 2014). Having preconceived judgements will not help secure a positive climate. As Norman Vincent Peale (1982) points out, confidence depends on the internal thoughts that occupy your mind regularly – if you think negatively and feel defeated, then you will be defeated. Think positively and you are more likely to succeed. If you let those staffroom conversations cloud your thoughts, then you are going to limit your success rate with these learners. Be positive, and lead with warmth and care, not with anger and frustration. Use your resolute optimism to encourage contagious impacts around you. Research shows us that smiling is infectious and increases trust and can greatly alter people's minds and attitudes in a positive way, making it incredibly powerful (Hattie & Yates, 2014). Now this doesn't mean that you need to give over-the-top gestures of outpouring love, but just show the learners that you care, that you are interested and bothered about them. Don't be fake with it, but drip feed that interest and attention over time – don't give up too soon and pull away that hand. Be consistent. I know it can feel hopeless at times but be consistent through the hardship and you will break through most of your tougher learners.

You cannot control a learner's behaviour; sometimes they can explode unexpectedly with little warning. However, how you respond to their behaviour is what will have a lasting impression. Many times, I would come home beside myself because a teenager said some horrendous insult, muttered under their breath, as I walked away – only to find the next day they had completely forgotten what had happened in the heat of the moment and greeted me with a huge smile. I learnt very quickly that a lot of the times, it was not a personal attack on me; I just happened to be caught in the moment. Children are very emotional and often let this override their rational responses. What matters is how you respond in that moment. It is easy to be swept up in the emotion and be pulled into the heat. Early on in my career, I remember getting into a verbal confrontation with a learner. They were misbehaving in my lesson, so I thought I would use my wit and try to embarrass them – BIG FAIL. I learnt very quickly that teenage boys can definitely shout louder than me – I was no match for them! In fact, I think they found it amusing more than anything. And in that instant, I had lost his trust and respect! I felt ridiculous and defeated and ended up sending him to the Deputy Head, whose office just happened to be opposite my classroom. In that moment, I showed my class I didn't know how to deal with this situation, undermining everything I had tried to build with them. Emotional responses like this are not effective; what I should have done was put my ego aside and not modelled such irrational behaviour. My reaction was disproportionate and chaotic, which was not a good representation of how to deal with heated situations. How I behave in those situations is more important, as it becomes a teachable moment. It is so important to stay cool and calm, and not wobble on our own expectations. The reason I struggled here was that I hadn't established my expectations in class, and I allowed my behaviour to escalate rather than nipping it in the bud. I allowed the situation to spiral out of control rather than hone in on my clear expectations, losing my credibility along the way. As I mentioned before, learners like this often deal with aggression outside of school, my shouting back just reaffirmed their already distorted view of behaviour, whereas I should have stayed positive and stuck to my firm but fair management strategies.

There was a time when publicly shaming learners was the norm in schools, with the 'naughty child' being placed either in the front or the corner of the classroom with a paper cone-shaped hat signalling the letter 'D' for Dunce, indicating to the rest of the class 'this child is an idiot'. Charles Dickens even references this punishment in his novel *The Old Curiosity Shop*, published in 1841:

> Displayed on hooks upon the wall in all their terrors, were the cane and ruler; and near them, on a small shelf of its own, the dunce's cap, made of old newspapers and decorated with glaring wafers of the largest size.

We look back to these times and think education must have been barbaric. However, some of those naming and shaming strategies are unfortunately still being used, not quite in the same way as a dunce hat, but still designed to humiliate learners. How many of you have put the names on the board when a child is misbehaving? 'If your name is still on the board by the end of the lesson, Billy, you will have a detention!' All we have done is swapped the dunce hat for putting their name on the board – it is designed to do the same thing, belittle and humiliate. Why do we use this technique when there is no evidence to support it? At worst, you have highlighted their flaws in front of the whole class and labelled that learner in a negative way. At best, you have given that child a sense of notoriety and a platform to continue to live up to this newfound celebrity status. How many times are you willing to put up the same child's name on the board? And what is the consequence? You lose your break or lunch time having to follow up, and nothing actually gets resolved. Stop using counter-intuitive techniques based on the myths that have been passed down the generations of teacher training. Start having high and clear expectations that you expect from your learners and build in consistent routines that minimise chaos and maximise learning time.

What is your expectation

Imagine, it's the first day of a new academic year, you have brand new learners coming to your class. How do you want to be perceived? Initial impressions are important, and you want to model your expectations right from the start. How do you want to welcome your learners? Do you want them to casually walk in and choose their own seats? This is fine if this is your expectation, but 2 months down the line when they are coming to class late and still casually walking in, it might get a little tiresome.

I have seen so many different approaches to behaviour and teacher expectations over the years, and it really is surprising some of the myths and practices some teachers stick to, even though it is clearly not working – from the military approach to the hippie commune environment. I remember during my PGCE year (Post Graduate Certificate of Education), being told by one teacher 'Don't smile until Christmas'. Another teacher once told me that the only way to control a class is to 'demand authority' and 'never let anything slide'. On the other hand, I remember when I was a Teaching Assistant watching a poor teacher cry after every lesson because she couldn't control her small class of 9 year 8 learners. She brought a tin of chocolates to class and gave them one every time they sat quietly for 1 minute to do some work. I get it; in a school the behaviour can either make or break your lesson and eventually your soul. As I mentioned before, with teachers leaving the profession because of the behaviour of their learners, I begin to question why more isn't done in teacher training. Working with teenagers, I remember those days of feeling the blood rushing to my face, both from sheer anger and frustration, but also sometimes from embarrassment. You know that feeling? When, all of a sudden, the room goes very hot, and you become locked into a staring match with a 14-year-old, sweat protruding and you will yourself not to be the first one to cave. Is this my expectation? Is this what I am willing to allow in my class? Is aggression and fighting the best way to survive these situations? No! I learnt very early on that some of the toughest boys in Slough responded much better to firm but fair consequences, a bit of positivity and some caring. While all learners are different, and I can't promise you that you won't ever experience a tough situation in your teaching career (there will be many), there will also be some learners you just never get through to, but here are some suggestions you could try.

Creating manners

Albert Bandura did a lot of research in the 1960s on observational and vicarious learning, focusing on understanding the role of modelling in behaviour change (1963). Both children and adults learn through observation when dealing with a new situation; this is done by watching how others are behaving and imitating that behaviour. Observational learning is often used in Early Years where children learn how to play, communicate, and get involved in growing complex social interactions (Ledford et al., 2019).

When teaching in a secondary school, behaviour expectations can be very confusing, especially if there are lots of contradictions taking place in each lesson – Mrs Taylor makes her class greet her at the door, but Mr Matthews lets them waltz in as they please. Mr Mitchell lets them chew gum, while Mrs Davies shouts at them if they drop a pencil. You can see how that would get both frustrating and perplexing for learners. As Dix (2017) points out, we all have to deal with behaviours in a classroom, but when everyone is doing it differently, where is the universal approach and unity? In order to really make a positive change to behaviour in a school, there has to be a clear collaborative agreement from the top, all the way down. There needs to be a cultural shift in school where everyone is living, breathing, and doing the agreed policy so that learners can see what the expectation is.

Start with manners. Just think if every teacher greeted learners in the hallway with a 'hello' and a handshake. Imagine if all teachers stayed calm in heated situations, and modelled polite behaviour? It might sound far-fetched, especially when you come from a school where it's almost impossible to get learners through the gates, let alone shake someone's hand. But it doesn't have to be if it is a conscious decision for all agreeing to follow. That means, no more classroom gossip of negativity, but a conscious decision for all to have a growth mindset. You must lead by example so that your learners can learn vicariously through your actions, not just in the classroom but outside as well. Dix (2017) mentioned a school he once observed using what was termed 'Fantastic Walking', in which the learners walked down the corridors with their chins up, chest out, and striding with their hands behind their back – such confidence exuberated from them. The headteacher had introduced it when she noticed lots of pushing and shoving in the corridors, so with pride for the school and love for her staff and learners, she taught them all fantastic walking. As a result of this, Dix (2017) noticed that the school had visible consistency, where the adults were modelling constantly, and the learners felt safe to imitate. In the Department for Education's ECT framework (2019), there is a big emphasis on working with colleagues as part of a 'wider system of behaviour management' and 'Reinforcing routines', building a 'predictable and secure environment' (p. 22). Consistency and collaboration are the keys to success.

OK – so you might not be in a position to introduce fantastic walking around the school (yet), but you can start in the classroom. You are their social role model and learners are more likely to effectively learn through the actions you make on a daily basis. By being a positive role model, you will instil confidence, so welcome your class with a smile every day, greet them with a 'good morning' or a 'good afternoon', talk to them on a personal level and get to know them, build relationships, notice when they are not themselves, don't berate them for their behaviour, but teach them why that isn't acceptable behaviour. Building good manners from an early age helps to instil those behaviours into adulthood. These can be considered critical elements in building up trust and developing traits of reliability and selflessness. When you stand at the front of the class, your learners have more time to study you and make their perceptions based on how you conduct yourself. The way you deal with the class, move around the room, your relaxed body and use of smiles and eye contact, encouraging tone of voice, and how you deal with individual students are being monitored. A lot of time, the students are focusing more on your mannerisms than what you are actually saying (Hattie & Yates, 2014). Elisha Babad (2009) points out that although these movements and behaviours seem subtle and invisible, their impact and influence on learners are incredible.

Seating plans

First question – how do you want your learners to come in? When you are meeting a new class, you might want to start with a clear seating plan that you have created. You can always revisit this moving forward, but it shows you have set the tone with expectations.

Learners will automatically want to sit with their friends, so a seating plan often forces them to separate initially, but much of the research over the years has indicated a caution towards allowing learners to choose their own seats. This isn't a new concept either; Krantz and Risley (1977) argued that having learners sit away from others was just as good at increasing on-task behaviour as giving rewards. Back in the 1980s, Wheldall and Lam (1987) also found that more focused behaviour doubled when learners were seated individually rather than in groups. In 2012, research was conducted on the differential effectiveness of seating on disruptive behaviour with fifth graders and the results were that learners were three times more likely to become disruptive in lessons when choosing their seats than if the seats were chosen for them (Bicard et al., 2012).

However, while there is lots of evidence to support seating plans, the next question is how do you arrange the seating in the classroom? While Krantz and Risley (1977) and Wheldall and Lam (1987) discussed the improvements in behaviour when sitting individually, this was more in line with the 1970s and 1980s classroom, not really useful when trying to encourage more collaboration in lessons. With only a 0.01 effect size when comparing open classrooms to traditional classrooms, we know that within-class groupings have an effect size of 0.18 and small-group learning has an effect size of 0.47, which gets us thinking about the best way to maximise learning. Previous research done by Kobe Desender et al. (2016) suggests that when learners are put into pairs, they will more likely work at the same level of focus as the person sitting next to them – even if the task is different. They argue that the exertion of efforts is contagious. This could link to the Bandwagon Effect, which stipulates the tendency people have to imitate those around them, often where the saying 'hop on the bandwagon' comes from. The Bandwagon Effect becomes a cognitive bias in which the brain tricks you into thinking something must be desirable because others want it too. While choosing your own seat can help some areas of well-being, especially amongst the shyer members of your classroom, being strategic with your seating arrangements can mean that you are not just placing learners in alphabetical order so you can learn their names quicker – but you are thinking about how to utilise the bandwagon and ensure learners are allowed to maximise their potential (Figure 2.5). Similarly, research

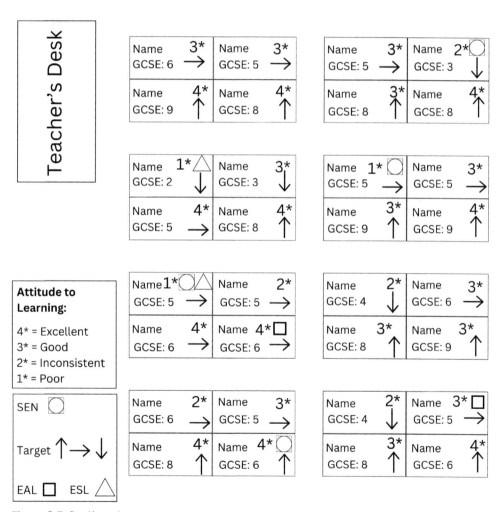

Figure 2.5 Seating plan

was undertaken to see the effect of pairing weaker learners with stronger learners in 2021 (Forrin et al., 2021). Referred to as the 'attention contagion', the research found that attentiveness would spread around the learning environment as those with shorter attention spans were more likely to concentrate when diagonally sat in front of a learner who was more attentive and focused.

Above is an example of how you can really utilise your seating plan to incorporate your data and make sensible choices about where you place your learners. Knowing which learners are on, above, and below their expected targets allows you to focus on your differentiation so that you can ensure progress is being made (more on this later). However, as Bethany Spencer (2018) also points out, seating plans are a work of progress; you are likely to change your plans as the year goes on, due to data changes/friendship groups growing/complacency, etc.

Routines

Ok, so you've mastered your behaviour as you walk around school, and you have your learners in the classroom, sitting in their designated seats based on their data and personal information. Now what? It is time to establish and reinforce your routines in a positive manner that is going to create a learning environment that is effective.

We all have routines, the way we get up in the morning, the way we get dressed; our daily life is usually following a consistent routine. These routines become a daily habit, something we just do instinctively and automatically. My morning routine usually consists of:

1 The alarm goes off at 5.15 am.
2 I scroll Instagram for 5 minutes before getting out of bed and heading to the bathroom.
3 Once finished, I come downstairs at around 5.25 am to begin my 30-minute workout.
4 Once completed, I head back upstairs to shower.
5 I brush my teeth.
6 I get dressed.
7 I come downstairs and get breakfast ready for the children.
8 I give one kiss to each of my three children before leaving the house to set on my journey to school at 6.30 am.

We are creatures of habit; most of us like order and routines to feel safe and assured in life. In an interview between Ruth Jahn and Professor Gerhard Roth (n.d.), a renowned neuroscientist and philosopher, Roth points out that 80% of what we do takes place automatically because thinking is considered time-consuming. By creating routines, our brains can conserve more energy and therefore minimise making mistakes. Changing all the time is hard work for the brain, which is why learners often find it difficult to go from one classroom to another. While the brain is pretty malleable in the early years, by the time we hit puberty, it becomes less so, which makes changing habits very hard. Relearning and creating a new routine require consistent practice and motivation, building in repetition daily (Jahn & Roth, n.d.).

What is your routine at school? Do you have one that you use with your learners every single day? Maybe it is something like this:

1. Learners enter the classroom at 8 am.
2. Learners stand behind their desks while they take out their planners, exercise books, and pencil cases.
3. Teacher checks uniform.
4. Teacher asks learners to sit down.
5. Learners open the exercise book to previous work, draw a line under, and write today's date and lesson title.

Now you might find this quite regimented, obvious, and boring, but as Tom Bennett points out in his book *Running the Room* (2020), learners will not grasp these intuitively, and so these need to be taught to learners and maintained. As he mentions, routines become the building blocks of the culture you are creating in the classroom, and therefore it must be taught, not told. Learners learn through doing, repeatedly every day. It doesn't matter what your routine is, or how many routines you want to include, but it does need to be broken down, modelled, and reminded constantly. Don't assume your learners know that you have to draw a line under the date and title, or that they need to write from the margin on the left-hand side of the page and not just randomly in the middle. We take these things as obvious expectations, but if they don't know, then how can you expect them to do it? And if you don't know what you expect, then they definitely won't. Set your expectations clear at the start and then reinforce them as part of the routine every day. Eventually, you will have created a habit within your learners, and you won't need to keep reminding them; they will just do it. By giving clear sequences of expected, modelled, and reinforced behaviours, it becomes easier for others to imitate them.

Some of the main routines you may want to set for your learners might be around the entry and exit of your classroom, the passing round of exercise books, your expectations when asking and answering a question, how you want them to get your attention in a lesson, how you wish them to move from one activity to the other (especially if you have set up workstations around the classroom), and what you want them to do when they are stuck. Seems like a lot, but again, this comes down to setting your expectations right from the start – the more these are reinforced, the quicker they become habits and therefore naturally a part of your daily routine. As Dix (2017) points out, don't start your routine by berating learners when they get it wrong, or haven't done what you expected of them; this aggression will not make for productive learning and will set the wrong tone at the start of your lesson. Your learners will make mistakes, and get it wrong, but that is where you model and reinforce – remind them of your expectations, 'Danny, is that how we walk into a classroom?', or 'Louise, that is not how we ask for help, is it'.

In a recent experiment conducted with 11–14-year-old learners, the research suggested that greeting your learners at the door in a positive way leads to improving their behaviour once they are in the classroom. Misbehaviour tends to be most prevalent during the start and end of lessons as learners begin to get a little restless, so it is important to intentionally practise the transitions in the classroom, getting students ready to learn (Cook et al., 2018).

Tom Bennett breaks down some great routines that we often take for granted, but need to be reinforced with our learners (Table 2.1).

Table 2.1 Classroom routines

Talking	How do you want your learners to talk in your lessons? When do you want your learners to talk? Often, learners are very good at interrupting your instructions, so by giving them a clear signal of when they can begin and stop talking, you will be able to control this compulsive need to jump in. You may also want to teach them how to politely speak to each other, how to stay open-minded even when they don't necessarily agree with what is being said, the importance of turn-taking, maintaining eye contact when someone is talking, and the ability to debate effectively. We cannot take any of this for granted, and therefore time must be spent on how we respond to one another inside the classroom. Reinforce this when they do slip up (which they will) – 'Michael, remember to wait your turn so that you don't interrupt your partner'.
Listening	Not to be confused with 'not talking'. Learners need to know when it is time to start listening, both to you and to each other. Teach them to make notes of what they are hearing or summarise the points their partner has made to ensure they can take in what is being told to them. Have a clear signal for when it is time to regain focus on you – 'Eyes on me in 5, 4, 3, 2, 1 – thank you'. Try to limit distractions to ensure they are focused and listening, 'books closed and pens down', and don't start your instructions until this is completed and all are looking at you.
Refocus	The trick here is to build on speed. You want to make sure there is a clear routine that gets the classroom paying attention quickly. Again, have your expectations set and reminded consistently – 'books closed, pens down and fingers on lips', or 'All facing me with arms folded'. As long as it is the same every day, the response time can be developed.
Answering questions	This is the biggest one I often see cause the most disruption, when a teacher asks an open question to the class and gets a million responses back, making it very difficult to regain focus again as a mini-debate breaks out. How do you want your learners to answer a question? Are you going to have a 'no hands up' policy and instead use lollipop sticks with their names on them that you randomly select? Do you reinstate you want hands up before you ask the question? Are you going to use 'cold calling' by randomly pouncing on a learner (not literally)? Hands up often show enthusiasm from your class, but you may find it is always the same hands that go up, so mixing it with cold calling is useful to ensure all learners are listening. Use follow-up questions to remind learners of good listening. Model to learners how to answer questions, using full sentences and good language choices. Give them thinking time before they have to respond so that they don't feel rushed and probe them deeper with their answers.
Activity transitions	Make your expectations clear when moving learners from one task to another. Set clear timers and ensure the instructions are clear. Make sure they walk from one station to the next. You want to avoid the rogue learner who decided this is a good time to go over to his mate to give him a smack around the head and ask him what he is doing. Are they moving clockwise or anticlockwise? How long are they spending on each activity?
	Think about how you are going to give instructions when you are expecting your learners to also move. Often, I see teachers say, 'we are going to move' and then try and give instructions while half the learners are already en route – missing the key information. Always give instructions first before giving the signal to move.

(Continued)

Table 2.1 (Continued)

Writing	As I mentioned earlier – don't assume learners know to start their writing from the margin, or that they should be writing on every line, not every other line. The worst is knowing they should continue straight after the last piece of work, not three pages later. There is nothing worse than when a learner tells you their book is finished and when you flick through, there are loads of random empty pages. We have to teach the younger years about finger spaces, and we have to teach the older years about being neat and consistent. Not only that, but how do we expect our writing to be structured? You can't ask a student to write without modelling what that should look like – is there a title? How many paragraphs are you expecting? How do you want them to show their working out? Glueing is the bane of my life – sometimes you have to physically model how you expect them to glue in worksheets. You will get the lovely learners who get out their scissors and cut the sheet down to size so that it fits perfectly, you'll get the learners who instinctively fold their sheets neatly and glue them in like little flaps, and then you'll get the majority of learners who stick it in upside down, wonky or on the wrong page.

Again, some of these do sound so obvious, and of course, we expect these from our learners, but this won't happen until you teach them this behaviour. Start by setting the routine, communicate it clearly, practise it every day, and reinforce it constantly.

Paul Dix (2017) gives five examples of Keystone routines that he suggests great teachers couldn't live without (Table 2.2).

Table 2.2 Keystone routines

Getting the class listening	Paul Dix is a big fan of using countdowns as a way of creating positive cues for learners to begin listening and focusing again. The faster the timer, the greater the sense of urgency and therefore the quicker they should respond. Using this opportunity to praise those who are doing as they are told is also a great way of reinforcing this positive behaviour strategy – '5 … great work Sophya, thank you for sitting down in your seat, 4 … fantastic group over there all are ready and listening, 3 … almost there, brilliant work, 2 … Noah, just close your book up, thank you, 1 … Awesome work guys, all eyes are on me!" The key is to then not start your next instruction until all have their eyes on you and are listening. If one of your students is getting distracted or still has their pencil in their hands, then a quick 'Alice, pencil down please and eyes on me'. Once ALL students are doing what you have asked, then you can begin with your instructions. Don't start before then; otherwise, you will end up having to repeat yourself numerous times. The more you do this as part of your refocusing routine, the quicker it will get, and eventually, you won't need to keep reminding the students. Countdowns don't have to be you either; a good timer on the board is a nice visual way of setting the urgency of how quickly you want things done – 'You have 1 minute to get your books from the side and sit back down at your table, off you go…' I quite like the musical ones that keep the tone light in the classroom.

(Continued)

Table 2.2 (Continued)

Setting work	Instructions can sometimes be tricky because without a doubt after your first few words, you will have a handful of learners jumping ahead and trying to start the task before you have finished your sentence. Dix (2017) suggests using a technique called TROGS:
	Time and Task — Let your learners know how long they have for the task and when the deadline is so that they can start time planning.
	Resources — What will your learners need for this task and where can they get it?
	Outcomes — What is the success criteria for the task? What are your expectations for the final product?
	Groupings — Is this to be done individually, in pairs, or in groups?
	Stop signal — Remind the class that you will be using the timer when their time is up, and you will want them to refocus again.
Reflective questioning	Using your teacher judgement, there will be key moments in the lesson where you will want to pause the learning to inject some reflective questioning to check for understanding. You need to be able to be adaptive here as you may have to intervene or redirect the lesson based on your learners' responses. You may notice one group hasn't understood, and therefore you are going to do some focused work with them for a little bit before you let them off again independently. You might notice that one of the groups needs rearranging. Dix suggests no more than two of these pauses per lesson, as you don't want to disrupt the learning, and merely use it as a measure to inform your teaching. Reflecting at the end of the lesson is also important, not just to gauge their understanding, but to get them to self-reflect on their own behaviour and self-discipline – 'How well did you work with your group today?' 'What did you learn today that you didn't already know?' 'How were you a good learner today?'
Success criteria	Set clear success criteria for your learners to follow, or better still – get them to help create the success criteria. This helps empower them and create a sense of autonomy with the learners.
Rule of 3s	Keep routines and instructions simple – stick to 3. This is where working collectively as a school to choose your key routines is very important. If a learner is going to eight different lessons throughout the day, and each teacher has their own expectations and rules, you can understand why they are going to start getting confused and unclear of what they are supposed to be doing. However, if all have the same foundation expectations in their classroom, it makes it easier to monitor behaviour across the school. My current school adopted the 3Rs as their behaviour policy – **Be Responsible, Be Respectful, Be Ready**. Simple alliteration is reinforced in every lesson for every learner from early years through to secondary pupils.

Classroom Routines

Class Rules		Consequences		Positive Reinforcement	
1		1		1	
2		2		2	
3		3		3	

Routines and Expectations

Step	Action	Expectation
1	Walking into the classroom	
2	Start of the lesson (Getting our equipment)	
3	Opening and writing in books	
4	When answering questions	
5	Regaining focus of the class	
6	Listening time	
7	Students walking around the classroom	
8	Packing away (how the room should look at the end of the day)	

Figure 2.6 Routines and expectations

If you are reading this before the start of a new academic year, it might be worth mapping out your routines before school starts (Figure 2.6), so you are very clear on what your expectations are going to be.

Praise and warnings

What you want to achieve in your classroom is developing your learner's self-efficacy, their belief in their ability, and developing their confidence in being able to handle any situation. This includes dealing with their behaviour and how they respond to what is happening around them. Remember, children have heightened emotions and don't always know how to express themselves. While negative behaviour needs to be addressed, there are certain ways of doing this that aren't going to humiliate or diminish their confidence. I have mentioned already the importance of not getting swept into a confrontation, keeping your cool, and using every second as a teachable moment. That doesn't mean we ignore bad behaviour. When you see a child is not behaving in line with your expectations, the way you respond is actually more important than the consequence you plan on giving them. Remember, often children try to get your attention any way they can, and often negative behaviour gets a reaction faster than positive – this is something we have to work harder to change. In situations like this, Dix (2017) suggests you should limit your formal conversation with the learner about their behaviour to 30 seconds – as hard as it is sometimes, don't get pulled into a lengthy dialogue with the learner in front of the class as that (a) draws everyone's attention to it, (b) wastes learning time for everyone else, and (c) has the potential to make you lose the respect that you have been working so hard to build up. Rather than focus on the negative, remind them of the good behaviour they have displayed earlier that day or week, and that you are not going to give the negative behaviour any more of your time, 'Come on Ahmed, I know you can be a much better listener, you did a fantastic job last lesson when you were the leader of your group, I would like *that* Ahmed to be in class today please', then walk away and give them thinking time. Even if they mutter under their breath, even if they backchat, hold your ground.

Behaviour usually happens in two; the primary behaviour is the initial action the learner takes, followed by the secondary behaviour – this is the one designed to draw you in and get a reaction. This might be their protest towards their initial behaviour, or them just responding badly to your initial response to the primary behaviour. Dix (2017) points out the pointlessness of allowing yourself to be pulled into this and recommends the following ways to manage secondary behaviour:

1. Don't get caught in by snapping back.
2. Refuse to engage with the secondary behaviour.
3. Give the learner a choice if possible; however, don't if this is likely to exasperate the situation.
4. Don't bring up previous negative behaviour.
5. Don't follow the learner if they walk away (unless it is a safety issue). You don't want to provoke their anger further.
6. Focus on the outcome – this is a teachable moment. Don't get caught up in the anger.
7. Ask questions and establish what their feelings are and where they are coming from.
8. Focus on the next steps to help defuse the situation.
9. Where possible, try to remove the learner into a safe and private place where they don't have prying eyes on them.
10. Go into listening mode; you don't need to give them a lecture right now.

I have to deal with many behavioural issues with my 5-year-old son; he can be very testing at times and when the tantrum starts, it can be a big one, usually around dinner time when he decides he no longer likes the food he has eaten every day of his life. While my husband can get easily drawn into the tantrums and annoyed by my son's behaviour, I merely say to him, 'Noah, I am going to put your dinner here, when you decide to eat it, it will be right here for you'. I then walk away and let him come to his own conclusion that this behaviour isn't going to get a response from me. Within 5 minutes he usually stops crying and I watch him from the corner of my eye slowly make his way over to his dinner and begin eating, usually followed by a 'that was yummy, mummy' and a great big thumbs up. Same with your learners, don't be baited back in, because you will lose. I am not saying it is easy; to begin with, it is so difficult and you have to fight with every fibre of your being not to snap back – it gets even harder the older they get and the bigger they are. I once had to bite my tongue around a post-16 pupil who decided to scream at me in my class; you most would argue that at that age they should know how to behave, but again, I had to question 'why' were they behaving this way. It is probably the most stressful year for a learner, applying to university, and sitting some of the most important exams in their lives – can you blame them if they all of a sudden explode? Now, if I was new to my career, I probably would have found this very intimidating and probably would have exploded back, yelling about their inappropriate behaviour and bad attitude – but that would not have solved anything. Instead, I simply said, 'I can see you are frustrated right now, would you like to step outside for a few moments, and we will talk in a bit'. I maintained my composure and calmness and allowed them breathing space. Once they had calmed down, we could then discuss what the issue was and how we could have better dealt with that situation. Hopefully moving forward, they would remember this situation and know to get up and walk away to get some air before exploding next time. If I could see them getting anxious after this, I would ask them quietly if they needed a time out and give them the option to leave and refocus their thoughts.

When giving warnings, what you want to avoid is creating a power play – just like the wind trying to blow the man's coat off, children can be very stubborn. I have seen this happen in many classrooms, when a teacher is at their wit's end and their voices get louder and louder:

Teacher: Come in and sit down
Pupil: No, I don't want to sit there!
Teacher: Sit down!
Pupil: No!
Teacher: I SAID SIT DOWN!
Pupil: I SAID NO!
Teacher: SIIIIIIIIITTTTTTTT DOWN!
Pupil: NNNNNOOOOOOOO!

And what we have there is full-blown escalation and no successful outcome. When an adult shouts, the learners either find this intimidating or hilarious. You will be having a full-blown screaming match, while the rest of your class will be sniggering embarrassingly under their breath – and we have that hot face scenario again and back to losing respect from your class. What has that gained you? Other than a sore throat and a pupil still refusing to sit – nothing. Instead try to reroute the power play; start with not turning it into a spectacle. Get the rest of the class on task doing something before walking over to the learner displaying the negative behaviour and speak to them calmly and respectfully:

- *I understanding that something is bothering you; can we step outside and talk about it?*
- *I hear what you are saying, and I will try and help resolve the issue for you, but I need you to do as I have asked so that I can get to the bottom of this.*
- *I can see that you are angry; let's step outside and have a few deep breaths, then we can work together to fix the issue.*

Now I am not suggesting ignoring bad behaviour when it gets dangerous and needs to be dealt with immediately for the safety of the class. These techniques are to help diminish low-level disruptions; however, you may be faced with more serious issues, in which case you must follow your school's Safeguarding Policy. I have had instances when serious fights have broken out with the older boys, and laptops have been thrown across the room (again, in my early years as a teacher) and I had to get more senior help. In these situations, it is about keeping the rest of the pupils safe. However, calling the Deputy Head because a learner refused to open their book is a tad over the top and can definitely be dealt with by you in the classroom. The moment you get someone more senior involved for something trivial, you are telling the class 'I can't deal with you'. The key to more serious behaviour is to try and focus on prevention. We are not trained to deal with fights and crises in classrooms – we are never told in our teacher training that we may encounter this behaviour, and we are definitely never told we might get hit by a pupil (rare cases). But by having proactive approaches through our routines and normal procedures as well as reactive approaches such as consequences, rewards, and sanctions, we can begin to build a culture that discourages these types of escalations.

Michel Feely and Ben Karlin (The Teaching and Learning Playbook: Examples of Excellence in Teaching, 2022) suggest trying to use the 'least intrusive form of correction' which is the idea of correcting off-task behaviour issues in the least confrontational and disruptive way possible. This strategy helps in minimising disruption to the lesson, avoids on the spot confrontation, and helps improve relationships, de-escalating issues in a calmer way. They suggest performing the least intrusive form of correction by doing these things:

1. Use a non-verbal sign towards the learner who is off track. This could be miming writing or reading a book – think about your old charade games.
2. Use the 'Say It to See It' strategy and focus on the behaviour you want to see rather than the behaviour you are not seeing – 'I really want to see lots of thoughtful writing taking place at the moment', rather than 'I can't see much writing happening'.
3. Anonymously correct behaviour first before calling out individual learners – 'I am just waiting on a couple of students to start their writing'. If you are going to use names, make it positive – 'Well done Hannah for starting your writing'.
4. Have a private word with the individual learners who are still off task – rather than publicly naming and shaming.

However, if more action is needed beyond this, then you need to think about your consequences. So what sanctions are effective? Fletcher-Wood researched this in 2020 and looked at when sanctions are and are not effective. He argues that they are not effective if they don't happen immediately – for a learner trying to gain a celebrity status through their behaviour, being the class clown now far outweighs the detention they may or may not receive next week (especially if it is Friday). When a sanction is delayed, it becomes uncertain; the longer it is left, the less likely it will take place, and either the learner or the teacher is likely to forget and follow up. Often the sanction is sitting still in detention – this teaches them nothing. They should also not just be dished out in the heat of a classroom confrontation, as they are often given out of spite as a result of an emotional backlash. Therefore, instead, sanctions should be set as soon after the misbehaviour as possible – possibly moving of seats, notes in the planner, or an email home while the learners are working. Be consistent with your sanctions; the more you use them initially, the less you will need to use them in the long run, as the threat of the sanction becomes just as real as the sanction itself – and if you are consistent with it, your learners will know you are not playing around when you say something is going to happen. Make the sanctions productive – they shouldn't be fun, but they should be instructive – cleaning up litter at break time, cutting out resources for your next lesson, etc. Make sure you have a restorative conversation with your learners, so they know why they are there. There is nothing worse than having a child sit in your classroom in silence for 15 minutes and then saying, 'Off you go, don't do that again'. Have a clear escalation of sanctions as well, to ensure consistency and fairness – don't go straight to SLT; there is nowhere else for that to go then and as I said, that just says you can't cope with this child. Don't let the sanction slide though, whatever it is. If they don't turn up to your detention, follow it up the next day with a longer one, and if still not attending, an email to their parents, followed by an email to their tutor on the next offence, followed by their Head of Year after that, then escalate up to SLT. As a member of SLT, if I have to call in a parent to speak to them about their child's behaviour, I need to have a trail of evidence to warrant my conversation. I can't say to the parent, 'Because Mr Neal said so'; I have to show what steps have been taken before it has escalated up to me. Otherwise, both Mr Neal and I end up looking silly and lose the trust of the parent as well as not resolving the behaviour issue. Mr Neal needs to show how he followed all the steps. In conclusion, Fletcher-Wood (2020) determined that sanctions show the whole class what is and isn't acceptable and remains important when dealing with misbehaviour; however, sanctions do not work for everyone. If after three detentions your learner has still not changed their behaviour, then something else needs to be done instead.

While you will always have to deal with misbehaviour, regardless of what strategies you use, teaching about appropriate behaviours to your learners will help to minimise the need to deal with misbehaviour; the 'successful management of behaviour relies on far more than a set of strategies to draw upon when pupils misbehave' (Figure 2.7) (Ellis & Tod, 2018).

Just like with my post-16 student, you will often be faced with opportunities to develop learners' self-efficacy when dealing with a range of emotions (Table 2.3).

The EEF (Education Endowment Foundation, 2021) recommends using extrinsic motivations such as rewards and praise to address misbehaviours and encourage more positive behaviours amongst your learners.

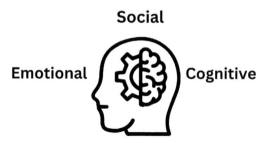

Figure 2.7 Learning behaviours

Table 2.3 Learning behaviours

Emotional learning behaviours	Learners need to know how to deal with their inner voice – often the one telling them they are not good enough, or that they cannot do something. Linking to James Nottingham's Learning Pit, learners need to learn to deal with setbacks and failures. They often misbehave due to their low self-esteem and self-worth.
Social learning behaviours	Learners also need to be taught how to form relationships both with the teachers and their peers. Bullying is usually one of the biggest issues with adolescents, so they need to be taught how to communicate positively with one another and how words can have consequences.
Cognitive learning behaviours	Misbehaviour can also occur due to learners' motivation and lack of a growth mindset. Teaching your learners that it is okay to fail and make mistakes can be shown through modelling and teacher-pupil dialogue. You also need to understand how the working memory and cognitive load work, because this can affect how they behave when they are overwhelmed or stressed in lessons. You will find that most misbehaviour happens when the work is either too hard, too easy or if the learner is bored.

Dix (2017) warns us to be careful with giving out praise. Often point systems and token awards end up being pointless because we tend to overly praise the students that usually cause trouble or reward the high achievers – meaning those in the middle are forgotten. Children are smart, and they know how to play the system; this doesn't teach them how to behave, merely how to turn it into a manipulation game. Try flipping the idea of naming and shaming and putting learners' names on the board when they do something wrong, and instead write down the behaviours you expect to see, such as 'working collaboratively', 'focused listening', 'effective debating', then every time one of your students showcases this behaviour, you put their name on the board next to the good behaviour. This way you are recognising the learners for their positive behaviour, rather than highlighting the students for the negative ones.

In a recent study, teachers of pupils aged between 9 and 14 who were particularly disruptive were trained on how to use behaviour-specific praise using the 'magic 5:1 ratio' between positive and negative interactions. For every negative behaviour addressed, the teacher should aim to give five specific compliments and positive reinforcements either verbally or through non-verbal gestures such as thumbs up. This was an experimental study, and more research is needed to see the long-term effectiveness of this approach; however, it did show that over the two months of conducting this technique, pupils' on-task behaviour did increase, which means teachers with disruptive classes could benefit from trying this technique out with their classes (EEF, 2021).

My personal favourite is sending a positive message home. Often, parents only receive negative communication from the school, a string of emails regarding their child misbehaving. If I were a parent receiving regular negative messages about my child, eventually I would stop reading them; there is only so much a parent can take hearing their child is rude, unruly, and disruptive, and how many times can I remove their iPhones and ground them? Whereas receiving a positive email from a teacher means I am more likely to be proud of my child and shower them with praise when they get home. A positive note means the child's confidence is growing both at home and at school and I guarantee they will come in the next day thanking you for emailing their mum, 'Miss, my mum was so happy yesterday, she let me have McDonalds for dinner!' With these regular messages home, whether that is an email, a postcard, or even a quick phone call, you will build up a relationship with the parents as well, so when you do have to send that negative email about the misbehaviour, they are more likely to be responsive.

While this will help with the extrinsic motivations, you also want to develop intrinsic motivation, which is crucial to creating resilience and determination within your learners. Learners are less likely to misbehave if they are intrinsically motivated. Carol Dweck (2017) argues that teaching learners to develop a growth mindset can motivate them to improve both academically and behaviourally. She also discusses how teaching skills like self-improvement and collaboration reduce bullying as it encourages bystanders to stand up against that behaviour. She also discusses the importance of praising a learner's effort rather than the person – 'Well done, you have worked so hard on this', 'well done for persevering throughout this task', and 'fantastic resilience, well done for trying again'. However, to develop growth mindsets, it is again about building a culture; it is not just about putting up posters around the school, but embodying it in everything the school does (Dweck, 2017).

ECT should note that it is normal for you guys to have more issues than more experienced teachers because a lot of these strategies take time to perfect and build your own confidence. Please do not feel afraid to ask for help and be willing to try different approaches. What I have learned over the years is that one strategy that works well in one class may not work in another – it is not a one-size-fits-all approach. When you are anxious, your learners will pick up on this, which is why the newer you are, the more you might struggle with behaviour management. But you have to ignore the small voice in your head filling you with doubts and stand strong. Even experienced teachers learn to mask their fears and anxiety, and just get better at blagging confidence.

Fairness and consistency

Suggesting a change of attitude to behaviour management and providing examples is all well and good, but it has to be consistent and fair. This goes back to what I was saying before – what are your expectations? Be clear in yourself first before you start introducing them to your learners. Then stick to it! Don't create a counter-intuitive classroom full of contradictions; if you say something – mean it! Ignore those myths of never smiling, stop hiding behind the persona of aggression and authority, start understanding the reasons behind misbehaviour, and start modelling the correct way to behave in situations. If you dish out consequences for one thing, make sure every child who does it gets the same consequence. The biggest one I often come across is hearing a teacher tell one of their learners that they will 'tell your mum', and when I follow up with this and ask how many times they have contacted home, the answer is usually – none. As soon as you don't follow through on your words, you teach your learners that your consequences are just empty threats.

Also, think about how you communicate at home – sometimes, when we are still reeling from the frustration of misbehaviour, it is easy to fall into the trap of becoming keyboard warriors and writing an email in anger. I can tell you now, the tone of that email is not going to go down well at all and that is not fair. I like to write emails in the form of a 'poop sandwich'. Always start with pleasantries, followed by the 'poop' which is the negative part, then finish up with a positive and supportive note.

Dear Mrs Jackson,

I hope this email finds you well and you have had a lovely weekend. Jodie has been working so hard lately, but unfortunately, I am just emailing you regarding my concerns about her behaviour in class today. I was a little concerned with her lack of focus, and on a number of occasions she displayed some unpleasant behaviour towards some of the other students. I have spoken to her about the importance of being polite to others, as well as the need to stay focused on her studies to ensure she is successful in her upcoming test.

If there is anything I can do to help support Jodie, then please do not hesitate to reach out to me. I am sure together we can help motivate her to be as successful in her studies that I know she can be.

Kind regards

I find that emails like this, while dealing with negative behaviours shown by the learner, are received much more positively from parents than when you go straight in accusing their child of being the devil spawn. Having a bank of emails like this makes your life easier as you only need to replace the 'poop' part to reflect what has happened in class that day.

One of the common phrases I hear from learners is 'Sir doesn't like me'. While we are not meant to be friends with our learners, and yes, there will always be that one that just gets under your skin and you'll remember forever, this phrase always saddens me. As I have mentioned, we are constantly modelling, and if we want to teach social learning behaviours, we need to be careful with how we model our attitudes in front of our learners. As Ofsted (2024) points out, we should be 'developing pupils' motivation and positive attitudes to learning, as these are important predictors of attainment. Developing positive attitudes can also have a longer-term impact on how pupils approach learning tasks in later stages of education'. It is not fair for a learner to have their self-efficacy diminished because they irritate us and so we eye-roll every time they say something in class. We are adults; we cannot express dislike towards a child, because then we are just modelling childish and bullying behaviour. Remember, our learners are learning vicariously through us and our actions. So, you must remain unbiased and fair – to all. John Hattie discusses how the greatest influence on behaviour problems were those that showcased a sense of with-it-ness or mindfulness; this has an effect size of 1.42. Those who can retain emotional objectivity are more likely to act quicker on noticing potential behaviour problems and interject sooner before they can spiral out of control. Dix (2017) points out that even the grumpy face of a frustrated teacher can make the amygdala put a learner into fight and flight mode. The release of hormones blocks their rational thought and therefore you have an emotionally heightened child ready to explode in your classroom. The amygdala learns from experience, so if your learner has a difficult home life, you might find they are more emotionally charged than others, meaning you might encounter more extreme reactions from them. However, through creating a learning environment that is safe, fair, and consistent for all, they will learn from their experiences and grow. Hattie and Yates (2014) point out that learners are constantly evaluating their teachers, not your personality, but how they feel you are treating them. While they might not be interested in you as a person, they need to find you acceptable, warm, and competent. It stems down to how you communicate and how you act, not your personality. You will benefit more when you treat your learners with fairness, dignity, and individual respect.

I am never going to say to you that behaviour management is easy – it is not! In fact, it is probably one of the hardest things to master and, as I mentioned before, can either make or break a teacher. But, like everything else, it takes time, practice, and for you to be consistent. Nothing changes overnight, and a tricky class may take even longer to embed your expectations and routines. I have spoken to teachers who have tried a strategy once and said, 'it didn't work', and therefore gave up. There is no miracle cure to 'fix' behaviour – as I have said throughout this chapter, it has to be learnt. Some are faster learners than others, but they still need to be taught it. Don't assume anything with your class – be clear, concise, and consistent. Dix (2017) suggests giving it 30 days to daily drip your behaviour expectations. He suggests focusing on 13 pledges every day to embed your expectations; however, I have broken this down to ten:

1. Meet and greet your class – start with a positive tone to the learning.
2. Make your learners feel valued and safe in your classroom.
3. Send positive notes home.
4. Introduce a recognition board to counteract the urge to write names for negative behaviour.
5. Keep your rules simple and easy to follow.
6. Do not shout (even when pushed).
7. Highlight the positive behaviour first (think the 5:1 ratio).
8. Don't allow negative behaviour to become the centre of attention.
9. Use a 30-second intervention to stop yourself from getting dragged into secondary behaviour.
10. Celebrate mistakes and build intrinsic motivations in your classroom.

Chapter Summary

- Set clear classroom routines and expectations to help manage your learner's behaviour.
- Use positive reinforcements to engage your learners in the lesson to avoid increased behavioural issues.
- Encourage a growth mindset and see challenging behaviour as an opportunity for development.
- Be consistent in your approach.

References

Babad, E. (2009). Teaching and nonverbal behaviour in the classroom. In L. J. Saha & A. G. Dworkin (Eds.), *International handbook of research on teachers and teaching*. Springer. https://doi.org/10.1007/978-0-387-73317-3_52

Bandura, A., Ross, D., & Ross, S. A. (1963). Vicarious reinforcement and imitative learning. *Journal of Abnormal and Social Psychology, 67*(6), 601–607. https://doi.org/10.1037/h0045550

Bennett, T. (2020). *Running the room: The teacher's guide to behaviour*. John Catt Educational.

Bicard, D. F., Ervin, A., Bicard, S. C., & Baylot-Casey, L. (2012). Differential effects of seating arrangements on disruptive behavior of fifth grade students during independent seatwork. *Journal of Applied Behaviour Analysis, 45*(2), 407–411. https://doi.org/10.1901/jaba.2012.45-407

Cook, C. R., Fiat, A., Larson, M., Daikos, C., Slemrod, T., Holland, E. A., Thayer, A. J., & Renshaw, T. (2018). Positive greetings at the door: Evaluation of a low-cost, high-yield proactive classroom management strategy. *Journal of Positive Behavior Interventions, 20*(3), 149–159. https://doi.org/10.1177/1098300717753831

Department for Education (2018, March). *Factors affecting teacher retention: Qualitative investigation research report*. https://assets.publishing.service.gov.uk/media/5aa15d24e5274a53c0b29341/Factors_affecting_teacher_retention_-_qualitative_investigation.pdf

Department for Education (2019, January). *Early career framework*. https://assets.publishing.service.gov.uk/media/60795936d3bf7f400b462d74/Early-Career_Framework_April_2021.pdf

Desender, K., Beurms, S., & Van den Bussche, E. (2016). Is mental effort exertion contagious? *Psychonomic Bulletin & Review, 23*(2), 624–631. https://doi.org/10.3758/s13423-015-0923-3

Dickens, C. (1841). *The old curiosity shop*. Chapman and Hall.

Dix, P. (2017). *When the adults change everything changes: Seismic shifts in school behaviour*. Independent Thinking Press.

Dweck, C. S. (2017). *Mindset: Changing the way you think to fulfil your potential*. Robinson.

Education Endowment Foundation (EEF) (2021, October 27). *Improving behaviour in schools*. https://d2tic4wvo1iusb.cloudfront.net/production/eef-guidance-reports/behaviour/EEF_Improving_behaviour_in_schools_Report.pdf?v=1731214741

Ellis, S., & Tod, J. (2018). *Behaviour for learning: Promoting positive relationships in the classroom*. Routledge. https://doi.org/10.4324/9781315232256

Fastiggi, W. (2019). The Three Pillars of Successful Behaviour Management. *Technology for Learners*. https://technologyforlearners.com/best-behaviour-management-strategies/

Feely, M., & Karlin, B. (2022). *The teaching and learning playbook: Examples of excellence in teaching*. Routledge.

Fletcher-Wood, H. (2020, March 1). *When do detentions work?* Improving Teaching. https://improvingteaching.co.uk/2020/03/01/when-do-detentions-work/

Forrin, N. D., Huynh, A. C., Smith, A. C., Cyr, E. N., McLean, D. B., Siklos-Whillans, J., Risko, E. F., Smilek, D., & Macleod, C. M. (2021). Attention spreads between students in a learning environment. *Journal of Experimental Psychology: Applied, 27*(2), 276–291. https://doi.org/10.1037/xap0000341

Hattie, J. (2023). *Visible learning: the sequel: A synthesis of over 2,100 meta-analyses relating to achievement*. Routledge.

Hattie, J., & Yates, G. (2014). *Visible learning and the science of how we learn*. Routledge.

Jahn, T. R., & Roth, G. (n.d.). Habits and Brain Research. *Sanitas*. https://www.sanitas.com/en/magazine/living-together-today/our-brains-love-habit.html

Krantz, P. J., & Risley, T. R. (1977). Behavioral ecology in the classroom. In D. K. O'Leary & S. G. O'Leary (Eds.), *Classroom management: The successful use of behavior modification* (pp. 349–366). Pergamon.

Ledford, J. R., Lane, J. D., & Barton, E. E. (2019). *Methods for teaching in early education: Contexts for inclusive classrooms*. Routledge.

Ofsted (2024, September 16). *Schools inspection handbook*. Gov.UK. https://www.gov.uk/government/publications/school-inspection-handbook-eif/school-inspection-handbook-for-september-2023

Peale, N. V. (1982). *The power of positive thinking*. Fawcett Crest.

Rosenthal, R., & Babad, E. Y. (1985). Pygmalion in the gymnasium. *Educational Leadership, 43*(1), 36–39. https://files.ascd.org/staticfiles/ascd/pdf/journals/ed_lead/el_198509_rosenthal.pdf

Schools Week (2023). *Record rate of teacher departures as 40,000 leave sector last year*. https://schoolsweek.co.uk/record-rate-of-teacher-departures-as-40000-leave-sector-last-year/#:~:text=Among%20newly%2Dqualified%20teachers%2C%2012.8,17.3%20to%2019.9%20per%20cent

Spencer, B. (2018, March 6). The benefits seating plans can have in your classroom. *The Satchel Blog*. https://blog.teamsatchel.com/the-benefits-of-seating-plans-for-students#:~:text=How%20and%20where%20students%20are,choosing%20where%20they%20sit%20themselves.

Whalen-Harris, R. (2023). The benefits of positive thinking: surrounding yourself with positivity. *One-Eighty*. https://www.one-eighty.org/news/the-importance-of-surrounding-yourself-with-positivity/

Wheldall, K., & Lam, Y. (1987). Rows versus tables: II. The effects of two classroom seating arrangements on classroom disruption rate, on-task behaviour and teacher behaviour in three special school classes. *Educational Psychology, 7*, 303–312. https://doi.org/10.1080/0144341870070405

3 Be clear and know your purpose

Fail to plan, then plan to fail

Ok, so you've set up your routines and you have your learners sitting relatively well (give or take a few bum wrigglers, and a couple of dropped pencils on the floor). Once those behaviour management strategies are in place, you are finally ready to start the flow of learning. While your students might not be waiting with bated breath (especially not the 16-year-olds who are still grumbling about having to get up early in the mornings), they do want to learn. This is where the challenge of instructional strategies comes into place. Hattie gives teacher clarity an effect size of 0.84 when it comes to positively impacting the achievement of learners (Corwin, 2024). As I mentioned in my previous chapter, fairness in the classroom, when teaching is organised and forthright, is so important as learners are clear on what the expectations are allowing them to work more effectively with a stronger sense of their own progress (Corwin, 2024). The decisions you make in the classroom can have a significant impact on achievement (Danielson, 2002).

One of the key areas I notice in lessons is the clarity in which instructions are being given – if the teacher is not exactly clear on what their expectation is, then this comes across in their unclear instructions. If you are not sure, then your learners will have no idea, which ultimately determines whether your lesson will be a success or not (Ur, 1996). We already know that learners are observing you to determine if you can be trusted and judging your level of competency (no pressure), and there has been some research that says learners believe that a teacher's ability to give clear explanations is one of the most significant qualities of a 'good' teacher (Wragg & Wood, 1984). The idea of giving clear instructions is by no means a new concept; in 1986 Chilcoat and Stahl published a framework for giving clear instructions to a class, in which they suggested keeping your sentences short and precise, avoiding terms like 'some' and 'a few', as learners can often struggle to quantify what you actually mean here. When instructions are not crystal clear, you may find some learners taking longer on one task than you expected, while others will rush through thinking they have finished and will then fill the time with off-task behaviour. How many times have you set a

DOI: 10.4324/9781003482123-3

task that you envision taking at least 15 minutes to complete, and you have that one learner chatting away off-task:

Teacher: 'Jack, what are you doing?'
Jack: 'I've finished Miss!'
Teacher: 'Already?'

Then when you look at his work, it is messy and rushed, and while, yes, he has finished, it is nothing like what you had expected for the finished product. Michael Feely and Ben Karlin (2022) suggest using the 'Say It to See It' technique, in which the teacher is clear and precise with their instruction while using positive reinforcement to recognise those getting it right and help encourage others to follow suit. They break this down into four actions (Table 3.1).

Clear instructions, whether for reinforcing a behaviour or introducing tasks in the lesson, are the fundamental parts of ensuring you are successful. While ever we are vague and unclear, we are inviting off-task behaviour, leading to that lack of consistency I discussed in my previous chapter.

So, let's break down a typical lesson into sections and see how high-quality instruction throughout can help minimise off-task behaviour and improve learner engagement and progress. This is why lesson planning is so important – so often I have seen teachers 'just wing it', and yes there are some of those who just somehow pull it off, but they are few and far between. Of course, time and experience will help you get faster at planning, and you will

Table 3.1 Say It to See It

Praise First	Remain positive, highlighting those who are following instructions by praising them first rather than correcting those who aren't. 'Brilliant work, this table is listening to my instructions'. While you are not ignoring bad behaviour, you are just not highlighting it straight away. We want to set the tone right; remember children crave attention – disruptive behaviour often gets them attention quicker, so it is important that we flip this narrative and give attention to positive behaviour to show that is the best way to get your attention.
Describe the Goal	Try to describe the behaviour you do want to see, rather than stating the behaviour you do not want to see. For example, 'I need you to be silent and listen to my instructions now' rather than '"You are not listening'.
Assume the Best	Often misbehaviour occurs because learners are unclear about what they are supposed to be doing (and yes, this might be because they were not paying attention to the instruction) but try to assume the best and check their understanding of the task and explain your instructions again to them. You will often see that light-bulb moment when they realise what it is they are supposed to be doing, and for the most part, they will then get on with the task at hand. If you go in aggressively accusing them of not listening, you run the risk of ruining that relationship you are trying to build – it may be that they were listening, but they struggled to process the information. Remember, don't assume your instructions are clear for all.
Explain the Purpose	Focus on 'why' you are doing this task in this particular way. Sometimes learners need to understand the purpose of why they are doing it, so reinforcing the benefits can help learners stay on track. 'Thank you for working collaboratively with your partner; this will build your teamwork skills in order to share ideas'.

build in the skills to be adaptive within lessons (which is the ultimate goal), but when you are starting your career, plan to the nth degree. Know the impact you want to have and execute this. So often it is the execution of the lesson where the problems start if the teacher wasn't fully prepared, or they were not adaptive enough to the needs of their learners. How are you going to start your lesson? How are you going to explain the topic? What questions are you going to ask? Which learners are you going to ask them to and how will you probe them further? How will you monitor progress and what will you do if this all goes wrong and everything you planned isn't working? These are all questions you should be asking yourself when planning your lessons – whether you write out a full lesson plan, scribble it on a piece of paper, or just have it firmly locked in your head.

Backwards planning

One of the best ways to really have clarity and be fully prepared for your lesson is to plan backwards. If you know the outcome of where you are trying to get your learners – whether that is by the end of the lesson or the end of the topic – then you are going to have a clearer pathway of how to get there. I have often looked at lesson plans and questioned, what is the purpose of this lesson? Sometimes the tasks don't match the lesson objective, or the success criteria don't match the outcome that the students produce. And I know from experience from my NQT (Newly Qualified Teacher) days; I would spend hours planning one lesson, for it still to not go as planned. Often lessons fall into the trap of being surface level and rushed through, rather than allowing for contextual learning. A whole lesson on adjectives rather than a lesson on the application of language features. What we want to achieve is in-depth learning, by having a clear understanding of the learning goals and then planning the steps our learners need to get them there. Grant Wiggins and Jay McTighe (2005) breaks this down into three elements.

Identifying desired learning results

What are the learning goals and expectations that need to be covered? By knowing the outcome, you can then start thinking about the steps that need to be taken to get to that outcome. You want to avoid 'teaching to the test' and instead focus on the values that go beyond the classroom. Think about some of those essential questions:

- Why are we learning this?
- What is the purpose?

Think about the phrase 'so what'? If they complete this task, so what? What is the impact? How is this relevant to them in the future? Knowing the 'why' is so important, not just for the teacher, but for the learners as well. How many times have you heard the phrase 'But when will I ever use this again in the future?' – I used to say it all the time about Algebra! If a learner doesn't understand 'why' it is important, they will struggle to engage with it. If the teacher doesn't know why it is important, they will struggle to get their class to engage with it.

Determine acceptable evidence

How are you going to measure the results of the learning? While you may have an end-of-topic assessment, evidence of learning should be a culminating occurrence, not just left till the end. Whether through mini quizzes each lesson, questioning designed to prompt critical thinking, or tasks designed to showcase the application of the learner's understanding and knowledge, these must be planned out. Many times, I have seen teachers go about teaching the knowledge of a specific topic, then the learners sit a test at the end, followed by swiftly moving on to the next topic. Were they ready for that test? Had all the content been covered in depth? As someone who has taught GCSE and A-Level English for many years, I know the pressures of trying to fit everything in, teaching towards the exam. For many years, I did this with a fairly average set of results – the learners achieved in line with what we expected them to achieve, but very few were ever challenged or pushed to outperform themselves. But that is because I was rushing over sections to cram it all in (anyone who has taught the poetry unit will understand what I mean!). My 'end goal' was to just have them sit the exam. What it should have been, and later became, was to develop their analytical skills to be able to apply to any questions the exam should throw at them. I began planning my questions better, rethinking the tasks I was giving them, focusing more on impact than knowledge. With a clear understanding of your expectations throughout the topic, you are going to get your message across to your learners better. If they are not producing the acceptable evidence you expect, then you adapt in order to achieve your desired learning results – you don't continue to plough through in the hope that at least half the class has understood.

Plan learning experiences and instructions

So, once you have your end goal, and the measurements you plan to use to ensure they are on track to achieve the outcomes you have set, it is time to plan your instructional activities and implement the teaching strategies you wish to use to achieve success. What materials and resources are you going to need to make this possible? What AFL (Assessment for Learning) strategies will you use to achieve success?

From experience, instructions get complicated when lessons are over-complicated. When we try to cover too much or do too much in one lesson, the goal starts to become unclear. I always break my lessons down by working backwards (Table 3.2).

Table 3.2 Backwards planning

Step 1: Outcome	What is the desired outcome of the lesson? What do you want your learners to have achieved/created/written etc.? For example, by the end of the lesson, I want my students to have written at least one sentence that includes an opinion, or by the end of the lesson, I want my learners to describe the life cycle of a frog. Visualise that in your head so you have a clear sense of your expectations – you know your class and what they can achieve, so align your expectations to what they are capable of achieving, but still have those high standards. You want to show progress in lessons, so how are you going to push them from surface level to deep level?

(Continued)

44 *Developing High Impact Teaching*

Table 3.2 (Continued)

Step 2: Learning Objective	Once you have decided on the goal, what are you then actually teaching your learners? What is the skill they are using to achieve the outcome? If I want them to create a piece of writing with opinions in it, then I am teaching my students how to 'apply' opinions to their writing in order to be persuasive.
Step 3: Success Criteria	Once you have your outcome and your Lesson Objective, now you need to be clear on the steps that need to be taken to achieve the outcome. What is the bare minimum your learners need to do to still achieve the lesson objective? Then what could they do to move beyond that? Think about those three questions – Where am I? Where am I going? How do I get there? I can write a sentence showing my opinion = Met the objective I can strengthen my sentence by using the word 'because' = Met the objective I can use multiple examples to strengthen my opinion = Exceeded the objective I can use the adverb 'however' to show a different opinion = Excelled the objective
Step 4: Modelling	Learners need to see exactly what you expect so that they can apply this to their own work. Do not assume that if you tell them, you want a paragraph with an opinion, using the words because and however in it, that they are going to know what that should look like or how that should be structured. Whatever you are expecting from them, walk them through it and give them visual examples. You don't want to just give away the answer, so model a slightly different version, but show them the steps they need to take to work through the success criteria – I would suggest having the success criteria visible on the board and referring back to it each time you have moved to the next step. The trick is to limit this to small chunks though – otherwise, you run the risk of having a 20-minute breakdown of just teacher talk.
Step 5: Task	Make sure the tasks you set for the learners are linked to the lesson objective and build them up to the end goal. What support might be needed? What resources are you going to use? Remember – don't assume anything, be prepared. Keep asking yourself 'why' – why are they doing this task? What is the purpose? What will they gain from this? How is this helping them achieve the goal?
Step 6: Evaluate	Throughout the lesson, build in opportunities for AFL. What evidence do you want to see at each stage to show they have got it? What questions are you going to ask, and who are you going to ask? As you get more confident, you will be able to do this naturally and in the moment, but as you start your career, planning these things specifically will help ensure you don't forget to include these. Key question – how do you know progress has been made?

When you plan your lesson thoroughly, whether that is scribbling it down on a piece of scrap paper or filling in an official planning sheet (Figure 3.1), you will be much better prepared for the lesson. You know your learners better than anyone – how do you need to adapt your lesson to get across to them what needs to be learnt?

Backwards planning allows teachers to shift from the role of 'teacher' to 'facilitator', coaching them to understand what they are learning and why they are learning it, as opposed to just teaching them knowledge.

Be clear and know your purpose 45

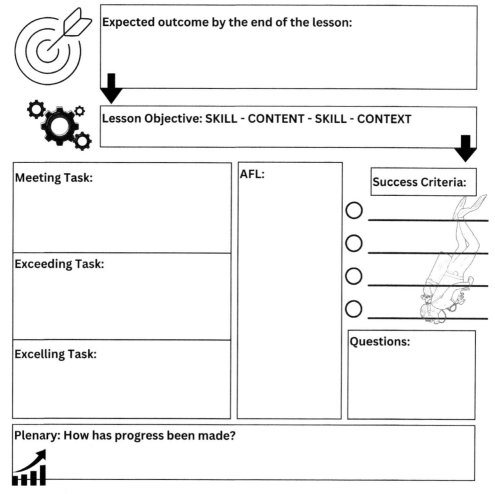

Figure 3.1 Backwards lesson plan

Lesson objectives and success criteria

As part of the Ofsted framework (2024), they indicate the importance of promoting progress, in which teachers should be accountable for the attainment, progress, and outcomes of their learners, knowing their capabilities and planning their lessons to build on this and reflecting on the impact they are having in the classroom. It is also important that learners are aware of how they are learning and take responsibility for their own work (2024). To do this, effective planning needs to take place, in which the teacher starts with the end in mind, using Wiggins and McTighe's (2005) backwards planning; the first step is to establish the purpose and goal of the lesson or the series of lessons. Often, we have a good 'idea' of what we want; however, effective planning means that teachers start thinking about this in more measurable and specific ways so that learners know exactly what is expected of them – this tends to be linked to the learning objectives. Much research has highlighted the importance of learners being aware of what they are learning and meant to be doing in a lesson. Eddie Gray and David Tall found, during their research into mathematical reasoning skills, that the higher-ability learners could work out what they were doing and why, but the lower-achieving learners struggled because they were trying to do something much more difficult (Gray & Tall, 1994). By having a clear learning goal/objective/intention, you are creating a clear criterion of what you expect from your learners.

Once the outcome has been determined, and you know exactly what you are expecting from your learners, you can then think about what they need to know to achieve that outcome. If I want them to be able to show their understanding of the life cycle of a frog by the end of the lesson in a written format, then I know they need to (a) know what the life cycle is, (b) know how I want them to show their understanding, and (c) know what that should look like. So, what SKILL am I teaching them? What are they learning to do to complete those tasks? A great place to start is looking at the Bloom's taxonomy verbs, as these help to create a foundation of active verbs that can be useful when constructing a learning objective. For those of you who are not familiar with Bloom's taxonomy, this is a technique that was first introduced by educational psychologist, Benjamin Bloom, in which he attempted to classify the different learning stages based on a pyramid. Starting with Knowledge at the bottom, Bloom believed ability grew to Comprehension, Application, Analysis, Synthesis, and Evaluation at the top. The purpose of this pyramid was to provide teachers with a common vocabulary that they could use to show progress through these stages. However, this was later revised in 2001 by Lorin Anderson and David Krathwohl to instead follow the chain of Remember, Understand, Apply, Analyse, Evaluate, and Create (Figure 3.2).

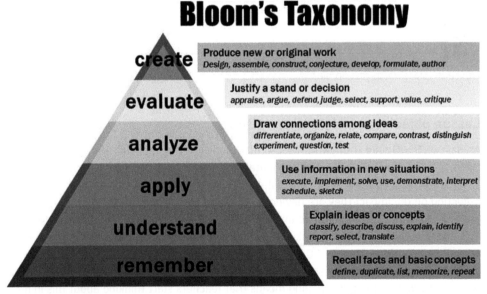

Figure 3.2 Bloom's Taxonomy pyramid of higher order thinking skills

Adapted from Armstrong (2010).

Table 3.3 Active verbs linked to Bloom's Taxonomy

Remember	Understand	Apply	Analyse	Evaluate	Create
List	Describe	Develop	Examine	Argue	Design
Find	Explain	Identify	Distinguish	Judge	Compose
Recall	Illustrate	Organise	Examine	Support	Develop
Tell	Outline	Solve	Inspect	Defend	Formulate
Name	Summarise	Present	Assume	Reflect	Build
Label	Translate	Interpret	Organise	Review	
Choose	Infer	Use	Experiment	Value	
Select	Demonstrate	Determine	Test		
Show	Remind		Connect		
State	Define		Deduce		
	Compare		Link		

While I have mentioned before in my previous book that I am a little sceptical of this hierarchy as it implies that understanding is a lower skill than applying and analysing, I do think the verbs used are helpful as a starting point for teachers when planning their Learning Objectives (Table 3.3).

Often, I see teachers create the lesson objective and then try to fit activities to that – sometimes successfully, but often they tend to have little relation to what the learners are actually producing. If you plan backwards, you have a clearer picture of what the end goal is, and then it is easier to create the lesson objective. For example, as an English teacher, I would often teach novels that consisted of a lot of historical context, such as *Of Mice and Men* by John Steinbeck (1993). I get to Chapter 4 which focuses on Crooks in his bedroom, which is also the stable where all the animals live – the purpose of the lesson is to analyse the text focusing on the language and structural features, but I could quite easily go down a rabbit hole and spend the lesson discussing the historical context of segregation during the 1930s. In this chapter, four key characters have all been ostracised by society during that time – Crooks, Lennie, Candy, and Curley's wife. Now both skills are important, and both need to be covered at some point across the unit, but what is this particular lesson focused on? Is it a historical lesson where I want my students to learn context or is it an analysis lesson where they are learning about tone? Most lessons range anywhere from 40 to 60 minutes on average – how am I going to maximise the learning during that time? If I have planned backwards and know that I want my learners to produce a PESTER (Point, Evidence, Single-word Analysis, Technique, Explain, Response) paragraph, then my lesson objective should be focused on applying analytical skills. If my end goal is to create a historical fact file, then my lesson objective will be to focus on applying knowledge. Peter Brunn points out in his book *The Lesson Planning Handbook* (2010) that being really clear on what the lesson objective is allows us to:

- Keep a good pace in the lessons.
- Ensure we stay on track with the necessary content.
- Avoid confusing our learners by giving incessant and extraneous details.

I always suggest breaking the lesson objective down to:

SKILL - CONTENT - SKILL - CONTEXT

Initially, what is the skill you are asking the learners to use? Look at the Bloom verbs - are they showing understanding? Are they demonstrating knowledge? Are they analysing, evaluating, etc.? Once you have established the key skill, then think about the content in which that skill is being used. What are you looking at specifically in this lesson? If you are analysing, what are you analysing? For example, you might be analysing 'language features' or 'structural features' in the lesson. Maybe you are 'applying' multiplication? At this point in your lesson objective, you have made it clear to the learners what skill they are focusing on; it is not an outcome, but a learning intention. Imagine your learners are sailing on a boat - your lesson objective at the moment has provided them with the skills they need to manoeuvre the boat. However, they then need to know the direction and destination to apply this new skill. This is where the final part of my breakdown comes in, the second SKILL and what they will achieve through using it. This is the CONTEXT of the lesson - the destination. This is where you think about your phrase 'in order to...' - by applying this skill what will your learners be able to achieve by the end of that learning phase? (I say learning phase because what they are doing might take longer than just one lesson - you don't necessarily need a new learning objective every lesson) (Figure 3.3). Shirley Clarke (2005) discusses the importance of not confusing the learning intention with the outcome of learning - often I will see a learning objective that merely states what the learners will be doing in that lesson, i.e. 'To be able to create a poster' or 'To be able to write the opening hook of a story'. It is the skill we are focusing on; we are then applying that skill to the context of that learning period. This way you are less likely to go off track as you can clearly see what the purpose is and how you are going to measure if the learners have achieved this.

When you are thinking about the learning intention/objective, it shouldn't be the activity the learner is producing, but instead the skill that allowed them to be successful in the activity. While there are some arguments to not include context at all, which I do understand as it is the skill we want to focus on, I do think that having context can help your learners understand what the end goal is, as Wiggins and McTighe (2005) point out, students perform better when they understand not just what they are learning but why it is important, which is a key feature of contextualised learning. What you don't want to do is have a learning objective for the sake of it. So many times, it is just there on the board, and learners write it down in their books, but no thought or discussion is around them. The learning objective needs to be deconstructed to show the learners what the success criteria are.

Once you have established the learning skill and the context in which your learners will be applying it, you can begin to effectively differentiate the outcome through the success criteria. As Dylan Wiliam (2018) points out, differentiated success criteria will determine to what level your learners can then transfer what they have learned. I think many teachers struggle with writing success criteria because there are so many factors to consider. Wiliam (2018) points out three issues to consider when creating your success criteria:

1. Is it task-specific or linked to a scoring rubric/mark scheme?
2. Is it product-focused or process-focused?
3. Official language or student-friendly?

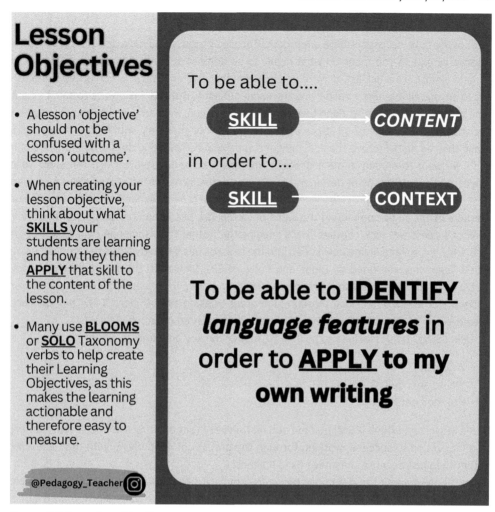

Figure 3.3 Learning objectives

Task-specific and rubrics

Coming from a Secondary School background, I am used to marking schemes and rubrics. Having marked many GCSE and A-Level papers over the years, it becomes easy to follow the criteria of 'best fit' to grade answers. Often when delivering my GCSE lessons, I would use these rubrics as my success criteria so that my students could see the steps that are needed to move through the levels. I could communicate the precise language of the mark scheme and reuse this criterion over and over again as I continued to work on a particular question or task. However, as Wiliam (2018) points out, a weakness of this is that while this will help support learners with this specific task, it is limited to only that. This type of success criteria is much better suited to summative assessments – they show learners exactly what is expected of them for that specific task.

Product and process-focused

A lot of the time, success criteria are product-focused because you have designed your lesson backwards and so you focus on what needs to be done to achieve the outcome. This would include almost like a tick list of 'have you included this, this and this?', which is fine when trying to ensure all learners as achieving the same outcome. But this will always to some extent limit creativity, as all are working towards the same design. Research is very conflicted when it comes to product-focused rubrics as to whether or not they help with long-term learning. While they do help improve the accuracy of a specific piece of work, does it build the lifelong skills we want to embed in our learners? Whereas process-focused criteria can allow your learners to see the steps of development. This type of success criteria takes more of a deep dive into learning and provides learners with the structure to expand on their work. Your learners might all be completing the same outcome, but based on how deep they dive, their level of success will vary. I always like to imagine that rather than someone swimming from A to B, they are instead diving down deep into the sea. For this, I would always recommend using SOLO Taxonomy, designed by Biggs and Collis (1982). Similar to Bloom's hierarchy model, SOLO looks at the relationship between surface- and deep-level learning, creating a clearer pathway for learners, working through high-order thinking skills (Figure 3.4). This way they are developing the process as they work towards the desired outcome (Table 3.4).

Using SOLO helps learners to be able to answer the key questions:

1. Where am I?
2. Where am I going?
3. How do I get there?

As McNeill and Hook (2012) pointed out, learners see that outcomes are achieved by effort and motivation to succeed, working through the process of deep diving with their learning, rather than just because they have fixed abilities.

Hattie talks about the difference between complexity and difficulty in his work on Visible Learning. I will often see a success criterion that effectively just provides learners with different outcomes based on the level of the learner, but really what we should be thinking about is complexity, rather than just difficulty. When we consider complexity, we are focusing on how the learner needs to integrate multiple skills or pieces of information, which makes the tasks more complicated to understand and perform – thereby creating a deep dive of learning as opposed to difficulty, which focuses more on the level of challenge that a task presents to a learner. Hattie argues that focusing on complexity rather than difficulty has more of an impact in education, as we begin to create tasks that challenge learners to engage deeply with content, promoting higher-order thinking and problem-solving, instead of tasks just getting more difficult but still surface level.

Hattie, Fisher, Frey, and Almarode explore the phases of learning in their new book *The Illustrated Guide to Visible Learning* (Hattie et al, 2024) in which they focus on the following three phases:

1. Surface learning
2. Deep learning
3. Transfer of learning

Be clear and know your purpose 51

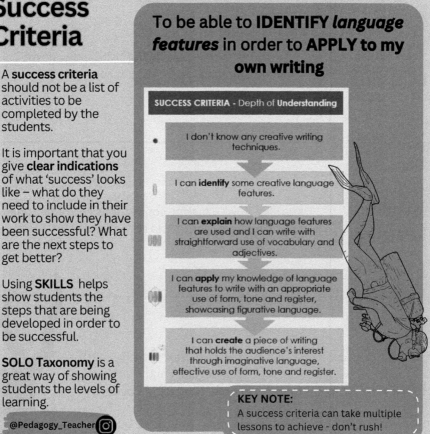

Figure 3.4 Success criteria

Table 3.4 SOLO success criteria

SOLO Term	SOLO Definition	Success Criteria Example
Pre-structural	At this stage the learner has limited to no knowledge of the topic and struggles to organise their thoughts logically.	I don't know any language features.
Uni-structural	At this stage the learner may have simple surface-level understanding but lacks the ability to explore deeper.	I can identify some language features.
Multi-structural	At this stage learners are beginning to make connections and start to explore some deeper understanding of the topic.	I can explain how language features are used to make our writing better.
Relational	At this stage learners are beginning to apply their knowledge to multiple concepts, piecing ideas together.	I can apply language features to my own writing.
Extended Abstract	And at this stage, learners are beginning to use different approaches to their learning, evaluating the process.	I can evaluate the language features I have used in my writing and make improvements.

Surface Learning	"Knowing That" – developing skills and concept understanding (acquiring and consolidating)
Deep Learning	"Knowing How" – making connections and organising knowledge (acquiring and consolidating further)
Transfer of Learning	"Knowing With" – being able to self-regulate and transferring knowledge to new concepts

Figure 3.5 Surface learning

During the surface learning phases, learners are acquiring and consolidating the initial knowledge being taught, usually through direct instruction and memorising facts. This is then followed by your learners moving into the deeper learning phases in which they begin to think critically, making connections with their learning, analysing information, and applying their knowledge to different concepts (Figure 3.5). The final stage is then transferring their knowledge to new and unfamiliar situations. This links nicely with the use of SOLO Taxonomy as they move through the uni- and multi-structural stages, to relational, and finally into the extended abstract stage.

Official language or student-friendly

Again, having worked in secondary for many years, we are used to having mark schemes provided for us, but, to be honest, a lot of the time these can be ambiguous jargon that can often be misinterpreted from teacher to teacher. When rubrics use more formal language, there is often very little difference between each step, with only a change in the synonym from one grade to the next. Having been an examiner for several years, it is easy to see how teachers build their own systems of how learners should answer questions, based on the rubrics provided, and it is often very different from school to school. Now the question is, do we give our learners these official language rubrics as part of their success criteria? I know I have for many years given it to my learners as a form of peer and self-assessment, and with surprising results. It is interesting how harsh many of my learners are to one another when following the rubrics and marking their peers' essays. I also think sometimes it helps learners to understand some of the terminology used such as the word 'nuisance' – it is a good teaching moment to explain what it means and then regularly refer to it throughout the unit. However, some believe that official language rubrics are often too difficult for both learners and teachers and so they like to create student-friendly rubrics. McEldowney and Henry (2014) created the 'I Can' statements from the USA Common Core Standards, as a way of making the standards more accessible to learners, teachers, and parents and allowing an easy tracking checklist for learners to see where they were in their learning journeys. Regardless of the type of success criteria you use, they are all designed to help develop your learner's self-efficacy as they begin to see where they are and where they need to go next. Another suggestion is to flip this idea to ask 'Can I' instead – allowing your learners to show they have met the different levels of success by actually answering the questions themselves.

If teachers are clearly communicating the learning objectives and driving them throughout the lesson activities, then learners know exactly what the purpose of the lesson is and what the expectation of them is. We should be holding learners accountable for achieving the learning outcome and measuring the progress that is being made, but this can only be possible if we have put in the stepping stones for them.

Greater clarity and clear instructions

Once you have planned your lesson and know exactly what you expect from your learners, you now need to think about how you are going to ensure you give clear instructions. As Griffith and Burns (2014) point out, the greater the teacher's clarity about the learning destination and the best ways of getting there, the better results they get with their learners. With an impressive effect size of 0.85, we know the significance of teacher clarity. Often, we can get frustrated with our learners because 'they just don't get it', and so we pass the blame on to them instead, but really we have to evaluate how much clarity we actually gave them. Remember, we can't just assume they have understood. Sometimes we don't realise that what we are trying to get across to our learners is not exactly what they are hearing, and so we must improve our clarity. Griffith and Burns (2014) recommend five strategies to improve clarity (Table 3.5).

Experience does not necessarily make you an expert teacher – it takes work. You could have been teaching for years and built up a strong subject knowledge, but clarity isn't just for the teachers; you need to take this and transfer it to the learners as well. The clearer you are, the sooner you can get your learners to do and apply what you have taught them. When you are not clear, they won't be clear, and therefore the outcome will not match what you had planned in your head.

Table 3.5 Developing teacher clarity

Being a model collector	Start building up a portfolio of past pieces of work. This will help you collect examples of the good, the bad, and the ugly. These pieces of work could be created by learners, yourself, or other teachers. If you teach secondary, they may even be exemplars from the exam boards. You can then use these to show your learners either how one should look or how one shouldn't look. I have often used these with the marking rubrics and got my learners to peer assess themselves.
Becoming a curator of models	Don't just collect work; really dive into those pieces and have a clear understanding of where the strengths and weaknesses lay. When you can discuss an example in depth, then you show you have clear clarity. The best way to gain this clarity is through discussing the work with other teachers – moderation is a great practice at all levels, as you form a strong understanding of what the agreed expectations are.
Conducting pre-mortems	The best way to appreciate how the learners are going to feel during a lesson is by conducting a 'pre-mortem'. Dissect the lesson beforehand to look for any potential pit holes. This allows you to pre-empt anything that might potentially go wrong in the lesson. Where could your learners potentially struggle or fail? Are there parts of the lesson where you might need to create more support for certain learners? Will you need to scaffold certain sections? When you know your learners and know your data, you should know who might need more support – so go through your lesson plan beforehand and start plotting where more clarity is going to be needed.
Becoming a black belt assessor	Again, coming back to that age-old 'backwards planning'. Have a strong clarity on what exactly is being assessed at the end of your unit so that you can plan your lessons to ensure your learners are also aware and can apply that knowledge. If you are a secondary teacher, I highly suggest you apply to be an examiner – become an expert in the paper, so you can better prepare your students. This way you plan your lessons to have an impact rather than just throwing knowledge at your learners and hoping some of it sticks.
Searching out your blind spots	This part really comes back to the importance of being reflective and evaluating our practice. We all have areas that we are not as strong at – come on, even superheroes have their kryptonite. The important thing is to be aware of our blind spots and actively do something about it. While ever we allow our blind spots to continue to get in the way, we will never truly be effective teachers. Maybe you are too fast with your pace, maybe you are too slow, or maybe some of your subject knowledge isn't always as strong (Shakespeare is definitely my weakest area). Find out what it is, work on it, and you will start finding more clarity in your instructions.

The way learners process information is not always as straightforward as just listening to instructions. The more you include in your instruction, the sooner you will lose your learners along the way, especially young children. Think about this instruction:

Jack, open your book to page 79, find task number 4 and answer questions 4-7.

While this seems like a straightforward instruction, it is actually four instructions together. Learners need instructions broken down into chunks for them to fully process what you are asking of them. As Dr Afzal Badshah points out, 'The human brain processes information in a sequential manner. As a result, the teacher must guide the students appropriately' (2022).

Table 3.6 Instructor clarity

Disfluency	When a teacher struggles to break down instructions into simpler examples.
Overload	Too much information is provided so learners cannot absorb it.
Interaction	Information needs to be adjusted and adapted depending on learners' level of comprehension.
Coherence	Leaving out redundant information so as not to confuse your learners.
Structure	How information is presented.

The Department for Education's Early Career Framework (2019) points out the importance of not overloading the working memory, breaking down material into small chunks, and reducing any distractions that might minimise attention while giving instructions. My advice to you is – do not give instructions until ALL are listening and ready to receive the instructions. Especially if you want to avoid repeating yourself constantly.

Griffith and Burns (2014) give a great analogy of giving clear instructions by comparing it to a magic trick. If I were to show you a magic trick that was a nine-step sequence using string, you would be amazed that it can be done, but without any verbal breakdown, you would struggle to understand what the nine steps are. You might get a conceptual understanding but wouldn't be able to conduct the trick yourself. I could slow it down and show you, which might help if you are a visual learner, or I might slow it down and describe it at the same time verbally. However, unless I give you the string and talk through it with you as you are doing it, many of you will struggle to get it right and probably give up. When giving instructions, it is important to remember that everyone learns differently. Just because I am a visual learner doesn't mean everyone else in front of me is. Bolkan (2017) breaks down five elements to teacher clarity (Table 3.6).

Just as I mentioned in the last chapter – don't assume that your learners will just understand what you expect of them (going back to my glueing in worksheets scenario!). To avoid misconceptions or over-complicating your instructions, think about who your audience is and how best to present the information you are trying to give. Mike Gershon (2015) highlights the importance of explaining and exemplifying your instructions to your class. With an average class size of 30 learners, it is important that your instructions are clearly communicated to them all. When explaining anything to them have a bank of methods to help get that information across, such as

- Examples
- Analogies
- Diagrams
- Images
- Flow charts

Using these methods will help to clarify, demonstrate, and exemplify what it is you are trying to get across to your learners. By having examples and images while you talk, it means your learners can contextualise what it is you are saying, minimising any ambiguity. If I say 'Underline the date and title', most of my class might understand and do it (with potentially varying results), but if I show and model an example and do it with them, ALL my learners will understand.

So, to summarise this chapter, your learners are going to make more progress when you are clear and know your purpose – we need to be 'explicit about precision-in-practice' (Sharratt, 2018). Have high expectations and ensure that you plan your lessons for an intentional alignment from start to finish. When you are clear on the purpose of your lesson, then your students will be as well.

Chapter Summary

- Your teacher clarity is crucial to ensure your learners are able to be successful in their learning.
- Recognise and praise positive behaviour and guide those off-task learners through intentional instructions that will guide them towards your more desired actions.
- Plan backwards to ensure you are clear on what you want your learners to achieve.
- Break down instructions into manageable steps to avoid confusion.
- Continue to assess and reflect.

References

Anderson, L. W., & Krathwohl, D. R. (2001). *A taxonomy for learning, teaching and assessing: A revision of bloom's taxonomy of educational objectives*. Longman.

Armstrong, P. (2010). Bloom's Taxonomy [Illustration]. *Vanderbilt University Center for Teaching*. https://cft.vanderbilt.edu/guides-sub-pages/blooms-taxonomy/

Badshah, A. (2022, June 12). The role of clear instructions in classroom! *Medium*. https://medium.com/age-of-awareness/the-role-of-clear-instructions-in-classroom-153be12aef3

Biggs, J. B., & Collis, K. F. (1982). *Evaluating the quality of learning: The SOLO taxonomy*. Academic Press.

Bolkan, S. (2017). Development and validation of the clarity indicators scale. *Communication Education*, 66(1), 19–36. https://doi.org/10.1080/03634523.2016.1202994

Brunn, P. (2010). *The lesson planning handbook: Essential strategies that inspire student thinking and learning*. Scholastic.

Chilcoat, G. W., & Stahl, R. J. (1986). A framework for giving clear directions: Effective teacher verbal behavior. *The Clearing House: A Journal of Educational Strategies, Issues and Ideas*, 60(3), 107–109. https://doi.org/10.1080/00098655.1986.9959298

Clarke, S. (2005). *Formative assessment in the secondary classroom*. Hodder Education.

Corwin (2024). What is teacher clarity? *Corwin*. https://ca.corwin.com/en-gb/nam/what-is-teacher-clarity

Danielson, L. (2002). Developing and retaining quality classroom teachers through mentoring. *The Clearing House: A Journal of Educational Strategies, Issues and Ideas*, 75(4), 183–185. https://doi.org/10.1080/00098650209604927

Department for Education (2019, January). *Early career framework*. https://assets.publishing.service.gov.uk/media/60795936d3bf7f400b462d74/Early-Career_Framework_April_2021.pdf

Feely, M., & Karlin, B. (2022). *The teaching and learning playbook: Examples of excellence in teaching*. Routledge.

Gershon, M. (2015). *How to use assessment for learning in the classroom: The complete guide*. Bloomsbury Publishing.

Gray, E. M., & Tall, D. O. (1994). Duality, ambiguity and flexibility: A "proceptual" view of simple arithmetic. *Journal for Research in Mathematics Education*, 25(2), 116–140. https://doi.org/10.2307/749505

Griffith, A., & Burns, M. (2014). *Outstanding teaching: Teaching backwards*. Crown House Publishing.

Hattie, J., Fisher, D., Frey, N., & Almarode, J. (2024). *The illustrated guide to visible learning*. Corwin.

McEldowney, J., & Henry, C. (2014). Everything CCSS: "I can" for K-8 grades. *The Curriculum Corner*. www.thecurriculumcorner.com/thecurriculumcorner123/2014/10/everything-ccss-i-can-for-k-6-grades

McNeill, L., & Hook, P. (2012). *SOLO taxonomy and making meaning book 1*. Essential Resources Educational Publishers Ltd.
Ofsted (2024, September 16). *School inspection handbook*. https://www.gov.uk/government/publications/school-inspection-handbook-eif/school-inspection-handbook-for-september-2023
Sharratt, L. (2018). *Clarity: What matters most in learning, teaching, and leading*. Corwin Press.
Steinbeck, J. (1993). *Of mice and men*. Penguin Books.
Ur, P. (1996). *A course in language teaching: Practice and theory*. Cambridge University Press.
Wiggins, G., & McTighe, J. (2005). *Understanding by design* (expanded 2nd ed.). Pearson.
Wiliam, D. (2018). *Embedded formative assessment (the new art and science of teaching)*. Solution Tree Press.
Wragg, E. C., & Wood, E. K. (1984). Pupil appraisals of teaching. In E. Wragg (Ed.), *Classroom teaching skills*. Croom Helm.

4 Leading the learning

Who is doing all the work?

Sometimes it can feel like we teachers have turned into performing monkeys – standing on the stage and playing the role of (fill blank in here) – every day it could be a different role. You start the day with the mindset of, "who will I play today? The evil Queen enforcing my rule over my minions; the lovable mother figure, endearing all with my charm; the wise old woman, delivering my speeches of wisdom; or the jester, desperate to make at least one student laugh. John Steinbeck, author of *Of Mice and Men*, once said that teaching is a special type of art because we embody the human, mind and spirit into the role we play, and we do it all without a script – we are the world's greatest improv. But, unlike actors, our audience are not always so willing to watch the show or be engaged in what we are presenting to them. We also have a goal to achieve by the end of our performance, an objective to be completed. So many times, when speaking to my children, my mother-in-law would say to me, "OOO you just used your teacher voice there", like I transformed into my character – clearly in this scenario I was playing the role of Police Officer. Now of course we would love to play the well-liked character, the Miss Honey of the show, but as teachers we can't just play one character because we have a range of different audience members we must appeal to. And we can't just play the fun, cool role because then we would just become the centre of attention, and that is not what our role is about. As Youssef Bounaji (2023) points out in his article, *Teacher as Performer: Using Acting Skills in the Classroom Stage*, teachers need to focus their performance on the learning outcomes, and keeping the lesson learner-centred, not teacher-centred. Good teachers can authentically adapt their different roles and teaching styles to fit the needs of the learners. They know when they need to be the main character, but they also know the importance of playing the side role. As a teacher, your role is to set the scene to encourage an environment where learning can take place, making the performance interactive and maintaining the enthusiasm and energy to gain your learners' attention. According to Tauber and Mester (2007), by animating your voice and body, you can produce a creative use of the space around you.

Ultimately, you want to ensure your learners are learning – but how do you know this is happening? So often I will ask teachers "How do you know progress was made?" and this often stumps them, and I get responses like:

- They were all listening to me.
- They completed the work I asked them to do.

Leading the learning 59

- They were able to answer my questions.
- They were quietly getting on with work.

These are all signs that your learners were doing 'something' – but none of these tell me they made progress, and who was leading the learning here? All these responses are very much passive behaviours from the learners. Looking at the teacher does not necessarily mean they are listening – I remember being a pupil being spoken to by one of my teachers, and I can guarantee most of my thoughts were on the mole on her chin and counting the hairs coming out rather than what she was saying to me. Completion of work doesn't necessarily mean progress either – was the work appropriate for their level or was everyone doing the same thing? Answering questions can be a good indicator – but again it depends on how well you probe those questions. Some learners are very good at guessing the right answer, so they may appear to know, but do they understand? And a quiet classroom is not necessarily a productive one.

Teacher talk

As teachers, we are often led to believe that we are the experts and therefore we need to fill our learners' heads with as much information as possible. However, there is a lot of research into the psychology behind attention spans. A built-in component of our biology, attention is present right from birth as a primal instinct to help us survive. As babies grow, they start to hone in on their attention spans and continue to build on this throughout their lives. Attention allows us to focus on information, create memories, and avoid distractions. Reynolds and Romano (2016) discuss the attentional systems in our brains, and how they advance throughout childhood. Between 0 and 2 months, babies develop the 'alerting' system, which allows them to fixate on things. This then develops between 2 and 6 months into the 'orienting' system in which they can apply direct attention to objects. After 6 months babies begin to stay focused for longer periods, which continues to grow as they get bigger. Kendra Cherry (2022) highlights some of the different types of attention we face throughout our lives (Table 4.1).

So, as human beings, our brains work incredibly hard to ensure we can have these different levels of attention and concentration – but it takes years to train and build up that type of stamina. Give a 3-year-old a task and I can guarantee they lose focus when something more interesting comes along. It took 7 years just to get my daughter to be able to sit and watch a full-length movie from start to finish. Research tells us that realistically someone's attention span is 2–3 minutes per year of their age. So, my question to you is, how long are you trying to keep your learners' attention when you are talking to them?

But why is 'teacher talk' still such an issue? This element of teacher talk is often referred to as the recitation method, following the IRE cycle (initiation – response – evaluation). This is a traditional style of teaching that has survived many centuries. I am sure if we all think back to our own education, this is a common method that was often used. When my dad tells me of his educational experiences from the 1960s, it was very much teacher-led with learners absorbing information. You either could do it or you couldn't – those that could went on to be academically successful, and those that couldn't went into vocational work. This

60 *Developing High Impact Teaching*

Table 4.1 Types of attention

Sustained Attention	More commonly known as 'concentration', this allows us to focus on one element for a prolonged period. When people have sustained attention, they tend to stay engaged until the task at hand is completed or a certain time has elapsed. Think about surgeons in the theatre; they must concentrate often for hours until the surgery has been completed. Research suggests that this type of attention tends to peak during a person's early 40s before slowly declining.
Alternating Attention	During this type of attention, you can shift from one focus to another, effortlessly. Think about carousal activities in the classroom; once one activity is over, learners can move on to the next activity without still being distracted by the previous task.
Selective Attention	With so many potential distractions in the world around us, our attention has limited resources. We must be selective and filter out anything that is not directly linked to the task we are currently fulfilling. When I am driving my car, I have to selectively tune out the arguing of my three children in the background. Similarly, when I am reading a book, I have to selectively tune out any other noises going off around me. When we are using this type of concentration, we need to be able to stop both external and internal distractions. How many times have you finished a page and had to go back to the top again because you were distracted by your own thoughts?
Focused Attention	This is used when attention needs to be grabbed quickly. In an emergency, when you hear a loud bang or warning, you stop what you are currently working on and refocus your attention.
Limited/Divided Attention	This type of attention is used when multi-tasking (something we mums try to do regularly). I watch my children, while cooking dinner and listen to a podcast all at the same time. However, research published in 2018 has suggested that multi-tasking is not very successful as our attention becomes too limited (Srna et al., 2018).

method enabled teachers to maintain control over the learning that was taking place, asking directed questions to particular learners, and then evaluating if enough of the content had been understood and ready to move on to the next part of the content. But, while this method has been used for many years (too long in my opinion), there are many criticisms around it. Firstly, the questions being asked are often too simplistic; it doesn't promote active participation from all learners, and they become solely focused on obtaining knowledge. Therefore, deeper levels of thought and understanding are not developed. It is interesting that with so much research to show this style of teaching is no longer effective, it is the one that so many teachers feel most comfortable with and naturally fall back into doing. Dr Gage (2009) researched why this method has had such longevity and concluded that it has stuck around because it seems to have been successful in building well-educated Western societies, and the realistic demands on teachers, such as having a strict curriculum to cover in a short period of time (Hattie & Yates, 2014). There has been some research on the advantages of lecture-styled teaching, such as higher teacher control and fewer interruptions, but as I mentioned earlier, it doesn't promote deeper understanding. With an effect size of -0.26, we can

Leading the learning 61

conclude that this style of learning is ineffective; ultimately, the majority of learners will learn very little from just listening.

Clinton and Dawson (2018) created an app named VisibleClassroom, which is designed to record and transcribe lessons. In their database of 15,000 lessons recorded, it highlighted that the teachers talked on average 89% of the time, asking around 130 questions focused on content, and only requiring three-word answers. With teachers talking so much, where is the attention being spent? How do you know that your learners (a) understand what you are saying and (b) how do you know they are processing the information correctly? The more we talk, the more we are doing all the thinking, and our learners are just passive. And while learners can take in more information as they get older, it is very boring. Think about your old University lectures – 9 a.m. start, sat in a giant room, listening for 1 hour to the lecturer reel off facts and information that you are expected to make notes on. With all the goodwill and attention in the world, you are not retaining all that information, even worse when you've had a late evening the night before! And that is when we are 18-year-olds; how much harder is that the younger your learners are! Think about the old quote from Confucius – "I hear, and I forget. I see and I remember. I do and I understand." The longer you are talking at your learners, the more likely they are to forget what they have heard. Training them on notetaking will definitely help, but the younger your learners are, the more difficult they will find retaining all the information you are trying to give them. Hermann Ebbinghaus' 'forgetting curve' (Figure 4.1) clearly shows us that retention of information is dramatically deceased after receiving it.

It is important that you think about your teacher talk in class – because 20 minutes after your learners' have received information, they can only retain around 42% of it. They are literally losing the information as you continue to talk. Unless you use retrieval practice

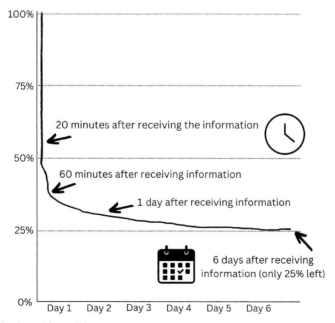

Figure 4.1 Ebbinghaus' forgetting curve

techniques, after a week your learners are only going to be holding on to around 25% of that information. The key is to chunk information into manageable sections, allowing them to digest that information and then apply it to an activity. Then continue to remind them of that information through retrieval practice techniques so that information can move from short-term memory to long-term memory. Hattie and Yates (2014) point out that studies have shown the most effective teachers will have good clarity, explaining material in short bursts of time such as 5-7 minutes. However, often our newer teachers have not mastered this ability yet, and so their instruction takes a lot longer leading to learners having to try and retain information beyond their capacity.

When our learners are overloaded with information, their working memory becomes very limited. There are two main theories about what happens during the time our minds wander. The first is the idea of ego depletion, in which our ability to focus intently becomes too exhausting due to the glucose (sugar) levels in our brains. Our brain will literally stop putting in the effort because it wants to conserve its energy for the next big task. Have you ever shadowed a learner for a day? I did this during my PGCE (Postgraduate Certificate of Education) year, and I can tell you it was exhausting. After being spoken at for, give or take, 7 hours, I was mentally drained, and that was only for 1 day. The second theory is cascading inattention, when the information being provided begins to overload the brain, leading to confusion. Both show how quickly and easily we can lose our learners' attention throughout the lesson (Hattie & Yates, 2014).

Cognitive load theory

As educators, I think it is important that we understand how the minds work so that we can ensure our classrooms increase learning while minimising the extraneous load on our learners. If we think about our memory, there are three main components:

1. Environment - the unlimited source of information around us.
2. Long-Term Memory - our own personal internal storage.
3. Working Memory - where thinking takes place, but it is limited.

Our brains are active all the time and constantly collecting information from these three key areas. For example, if someone asks me what I want for dinner, my brain remembers meals I have enjoyed in the past which are in my long-term memory, then, as I look online at my meal choices, my working memory retains all the different options so that I can make a choice. Doesn't that sound exhausting - and that is just thinking about dinner! Collectively, these three elements give us the ability to think. However, while the environment and the long-term memory are unlimited, the working memory only has a small capacity, and therefore often leads to confusion and system overload. The more we see and hear things, the more it seeps through our working memory into our long-term memory, and once it is there, it is there for good! The only French I can really, confidently remember is "asseyez-vous", which means "sit down", and that is because my French teacher started every French lesson like that from Year 7 through to my GCSEs in Year 11 (again, goes back to creating routines in the classroom). When we hear or see familiar things around us, our brain works together with the environment and the long-term memory so that our working memory can process the information more quickly. However, when we are introduced to new information, it takes up more room in the working memory, leaving little room for anything else. Once it has moved to the long-term memory, our brains begin to do what is called 'chunking'. As Oliver Lovell (2020) shows, when a child is first deciphering letters, what starts off as three lines on a page eventually becomes an 'H'; the brain chunks these three pieces of information together to form the letter. As a child develops, they start chunking information for all letters, understanding the different sounds followed by piecing together the words. While this would have once been a demanding task for the brain, through regular usage and chunking information together in the long-term memory, we get faster and eventually do it automatically. As teachers, we want to move as much information from the working memory into the long-term memory, but we have to be cautious of cognitive overload. When we add things like routines to our lessons, we begin building in that ability to automate; you will see some teachers only have to say the words, 'We are coming to the end of the lesson now', and their learners automatically close their books, put their equipment away, and get out their whiteboards ready for the plenary exercise. This is because that one phrase has been chunked together with the multiple actions – and through the regular embedding of the practice, it becomes an automatic part of every lesson.

Often, we take things for granted, because we are older and have developed our long-term memory, but you must remember your learners are still getting to grips with chunking. Why is it that they keep making the same spelling mistake, or grammar errors? Why is it they can't recall the information you gave them yesterday? The truth is, it is in the memory, but they have not yet chunked those actions together, so it takes their brains slightly longer to process all the information being given to them. Every time they learn something, it is new information taking up space in their working memory that needs to be processed and chunked repeatedly for it to pass to the long-term stage. These are called 'schemas', and it is our brains' way of making connections and categorising information. As new information comes in, we either link it to an already-formed schema or create a new one (Figure 4.2). The more knowledge we gain, the more connections are made, and when regularly used, this is added to our long-term memory – but if not, just like Ebbinghaus' forgetting curve, it will soon be gone.

John Sweller first coined Cognitive Load Theory (CLT) in 1988, in which he showed how our working memory only holds onto a small amount of information at any given time and, therefore, instructional methods need to minimise information overload to maximise learning. He came about this concept through conducting some seminal experiments with his colleagues on undergraduates at the University of New South Wales. During one particular experiment, he asked the learners to solve some math problems. One group was asked to look for a pattern in the problems, whereas the other group was not given this information. While they were still able to successfully solve the problems, it took them much longer. As Greg Ashman (2023) points out, without having the rule to follow, the second group was blindly conducting a 'means-ends analysis', meaning they were constantly evaluating each move they were making and trying to work out if they were closer to the target or not. From conducting these experiments, Sweller saw how tiresome it was for those in that group

64 *Developing High Impact Teaching*

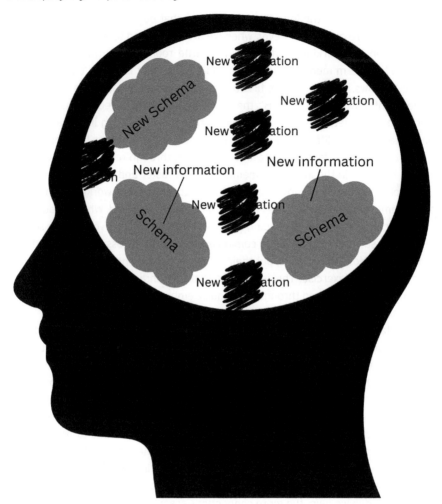

Figure 4.2 Cognitive load theory

that they didn't have enough mental capacity to notice the patterns with everything else going on. There is a difference between being 'busy' and 'learning'. While these learners were busy solving the problems, they didn't learn the key method of pattern finding, which would have maximised their learning further. While their brains were busy trying to solve the problem the long way, with clearer instructions, they could have found connections much quicker.

According to research, there are three types of cognitive load (Paas et al., 2010):

1 Intrinsic Cognitive Load – this is the challenge that naturally occurs when a learner is completing a task, especially when new or particularly hard vocabulary is present. Processing information is difficult, regardless of what the task is or how it has been presented.

Leading the learning   65

2   Extraneous Cognitive Load – these are the potential distractions that take place when a learner is trying to concentrate on the desired task. This could be when a learner is trying to read but there is a conversation taking place behind them which is distracting their attention.
3   Germane Cognitive Load – these are formed when learners use their working memory and create new schemas.

As you can see, the intrinsic and extraneous load can both make learning difficult for learners and therefore should be monitored as much as possible to help aid learning in the classroom, whereas the germane load is more conducive for learning to take place. Knowing about these types of cognitive loads is important, as we need to be mindful of controlling any additional pressure on the working memory (Figure 4.3). Really what we want to achieve is minimising the extraneous load and optimising the intrinsic. While intrinsic load can make learning difficult, it is also necessary for learners to develop the ability to process information better. Therefore, we need to know when to increase and decrease this load (Lovell, 2020).

When we give our learners a task to do through instruction, their intrinsic load starts working, filtering the information, and working alongside the germane load to create links to make new schemas. But while this is taking place, it is also competing with the extraneous load. Imagine you have given your learners a textbook to read, but the textbook also

Figure 4.3 Intrinsic load versus extraneous load

66 *Developing High Impact Teaching*

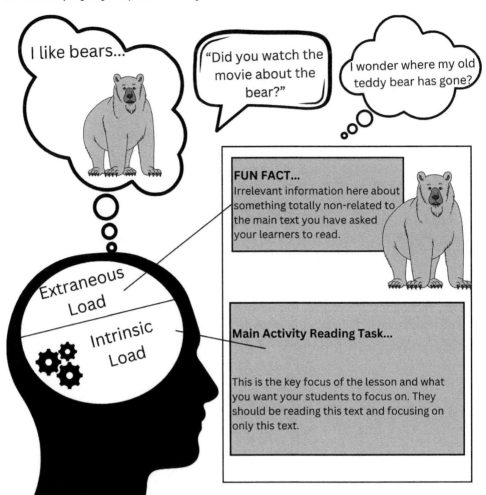

Figure 4.4 Intrinsic load competition

has lots of other boxes of information around the outside of the main text you want them to read – they are going to get side-tracked and distracted by the extra information (Figure 4.4). Similarly, if there are images that are not necessarily connected to the main text, their minds are going to try and make a connection by bringing up information they have already formed in the past.

In this situation, we need to increase the intrinsic load but minimise the extraneous, unnecessary information. In cases like this, sometimes less is more to maximise our learners' outcomes. However, there may be times when you need to reduce the intrinsic load, for example, if you were to give them a text that was just too difficult for them. While you may have minimised the extraneous load, they may still be experiencing cognitive overload. In this instance, the information might need to be broken down for the learners so that they are still able to work within the limits of their working memory. This goes back to what I was discussing earlier in this chapter, focusing on the instructions we are giving to our learners; remember their attention span and their ability to retain information is limited, and so we need to minimise how much we are talking. I don't know about you, but I am already exhausted trying to explain how the mind works – imagine your poor learners actually experiencing this in your lessons! Learning is hard work!

Lovell (2020) suggests pre-teaching as a strategy to help optimise intrinsic load. This could be through pre-teaching new vocabulary by using Alex Quigley's SEEC technique – select, explain, explore and consolidate (2018). In this technique, you select the keywords you know are going to be in the next part of learning. Once these have been selected, you explain what the word is and how it is pronounced; exploration could be then looking at the origins of the word and any synonyms that could be associated followed by consolidation, in which the word is strategically planned into multiple parts of the lessons leading up to when it is going to be needed. Similarly, you may want to pre-teach characters, events, and timelines. When I was teaching Othello to my A-Level Literature learners, one of my earlier lessons would be dedicated to pre-teaching all the different characters by placing information around the room and my learners would have to create a web to show how they were all connected. Similarly, I would start my *Of Mice and Men* unit with a history lesson to teach my learners the historical context of 1930s America. Allowing them to explore racial segregation and oppression during the Great Depression meant that connections would be created much more quickly when we delved into the content of the story and therefore themes better understood.

Another great way of optimising intrinsic load is using mnemonics. As an English teacher, I always wanted my learners to write good analytical paragraphs, but there are so many elements that go into creating these. To help support my learners, I used the term 'PESTER Paragraph', using repetition to embed all the elements they should be using:

- Point
- Evidence
- Single-Word Analysis
- Technique
- Explain
- Response

Collectively, that is a lot of information, but 'PESTER' makes it easier to remember. By creating a mnemonic, I make the information less taxing for the working memory. Mnemonics are used to initiate memory (Governor et al., 2012). They are useful because visual-verbal links are formed and easily retrieved (Scruggs et al., 2010). When a mnemonic is created, the learner builds a mental representation of what it stands for and stores the information so that when they see or hear it, they remember what it is.

With an effect size of 0.65, this is a great way of reducing CLT as it reduces the extrinsic load, making it easier for the learner to piece together information and store it in their long-term memory. By making connections through grouping information into smaller, more manageable chunks, we can overcome the limitations of the working memory and form those secure schemas in our long-term memory (Milenković et al., 2014). There are multiple ways of incorporating mnemonics into learning (Figure 4.5) such as given in Table 4.2.

1) Loci Strategy – Using places to chunk together key information

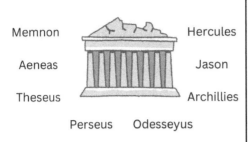

Memnon   Hercules
Aeneas   Jason
Theseus   Archillies
   Perseus   Odesseyus

2) Peg Word Strategy – numbering key words to recall information

MNEMONICS
0.65 Effect Size

3) Acronym/Acrostic Strategy

Richard - Red
Of - Orange
York - Yellow
Gave - Green
Battle - Blue
In - Indigo
Vain - Violet

4) Rhyming Strategy

30 days hath September
April, June and November

Figure 4.5 Mnemonics

A study conducted in a school in Oman measured the impact of using mnemonics in science lessons as a way of minimising the cognitive load with 212 sixth graders (Al-Maqbali et al., 2022). Using the Peg strategy and use of images, the overall results showed that when mnemonics were used, they significantly reduced the cognitive load of the learners. The learners who were in the groups that used mnemonics as part of their learning were able to develop schemas and develop learning efficiency.

So, we have discussed the negative impact of teacher talk and the effect of cognitive overload – we need to now think about how we can make sure our learners are leading the learning. Evidence tells us very clearly that too much teacher talk is counter-productive when trying to get learners thinking. Remember, we are not the performers – we shouldn't be doing all the work. But how do we ensure that our learners are effectively engaged and learning?

Table 4.2 Mnemonic strategies

Loci Strategy	Linking material to places your learners are familiar with. Once learners have thought of a specific place, they create visual images of the information they are trying to remember, linking them to the place they have chosen. For example, if I was learning about ancient Greece, I might picture the Parthenon and use that as my base for memorising different elements of the Greek lifestyle.
Peg Word Strategy	Imagine you are hanging information onto some coat pegs by the front door. The Peg strategy is using words/images hanging on pegs as a visual reminder of a bigger concept. Each word/image is linked to a number to help you memorise the order. So, for example, if I wanted to remember the story of Little Red Riding Hood, I might break it down into these images: 1. Red Cloak 2. Basket 3. Tree 4. Wolf 5. Grandma 6. Glasses 7. Teeth 8. Huntsman Through using these words, I can picture these images in this order and know that Little Red Riding Hood puts on her (red clock) and takes a (basket) of fresh buns into the woods (tree) where she encounters a (wolf) who asks her where she is going. She tells him she is going to visit her (Grandma). The wolf leaves the girl and runs ahead. Once the girl arrives at her grandma's house, she notices what big eyes (glasses) she has, followed by what big (teeth) she has – which turns out to be the wolf who is about to eat her. However, she is saved by a trusty (Huntsman) who kills the beast and saves Little Red Riding Hood and her grandma. You might also use it to help remember your shopping lists, using a rhyming method: 1. Bun (burgers) 2. Loo (toilet rolls) 3. Tea 4. Sore (band aids) 5. Hive (honey) This technique can help memorise lists, events, or even quotes – it is a form of chunking information.
Linking Chain Strategy	Very similar to the Peg method, the linking chain is designed to use images that link together to tell a bigger story. It is often told in the form of a story to help you memorise. For example, say I wanted to remember the events of the Great Fire of London; I might piece it together like this: One day I was really hungry (bakery). While I was looking for food, I started to feel very hot (fire). I decided to skip down the path (fire spreading) touching the long grass as I went (thatch roofs catching fire). Eventually, I reached the river for a swim (fire engines/hoses). I then felt much cooler (the fire was put out). This is a great technique for learners who are creative and like storytelling. Each part links to the next to further help them remember. When I was doing my

(Continued)

Table 4.2 (Continued)

	GCSEs, I remember my older sister helping me to revise atoms. She put it into a story like this:
	• Once there was a strong electrostatic force of attraction between you and your boyfriend – oppositely charged ions – this is called an ionic bond (you are opposites but attract each other).
	• You and your best friend create a covalent bond because you both are two non-metal atoms (you are both the same, i.e., non-metal, and have a strong bond, i.e., friendship).
	• But in comes someone with the same ionic charge (i.e., both positive ions or both negative ions), and they instantly repulse you – they do not bond with you and become your worst enemy.
	I was able to link the key elements together by turning them into a story to help me memorise.
Acronym-Acrostic Strategy	Just like my PESTER example, this strategy helps you memorise bigger pieces of information by abbreviating them into memorable acronyms or acrostics. Some popular acronyms are:
	ASAP – As soon as possible **BRB** – Be right back **ELL** – English Language Learner **EAL** – English as an Additional Language **ESL** – English as a Second Language
	Other English-related acronyms I have used while teaching have been different variations of PESTER, such as PEARL, PEE, PEA, PETER, etc. I have also used **SLAP** (Structure, Language, Audience, Purpose) as a revision tool for the English Language GCSE paper. Another popular one to help remember the colours of the rainbow is:
	Richard (Red) **Of** (Orange) **York** (Yellow) **Gave** (Green) **Battle** (Blue) **In** (Indigo) **Vain** (Violet)
Keyword Strategy	I used this strategy a lot when revising for my History GCSE exam. I would memorise key information by associating images with chunks of information. For example, when revising the 1856 Andover Workhouse Scandal, I drew a picture of bones; this represented the bone-crushing that took place inside the workhouse, along with many other inhumane treatments of the poor. Similarly, to remember the 1815 Corn Laws, I drew a bouquet of corn. Another way is by associating new vocabulary with something similar. For example, the word 'apex' is like 'ape' – so I could picture an ape to remind me. If I was learning a new language, I might think of what the word sounds like, such as in Arabic the word 'nose' is 'أنف' – 'anf', which sounds like 'ant fun' – so I picture a group of ants having a party.
Rhyme Strategy	Here learners memorise through rhyming, creating a melodic beat. There are some you might even remember from your childhood: • 30 days hath September, April, June, and November. • Never eat shredded wheat (North, East, South, West).

Student engagement

When I observe lessons, I try and do so through the eyes of the learners. I am not interested in what the teacher is doing, but instead in how the learners are learning. During this time, I will keep an eye on the clock and monitor how long the instructions are taking place, I will monitor the learner's attention and engagement, and I will observe how the learners are recording information (if at all). In one lesson I was observing, the instructions took 20 minutes with the occasional questioning taking place. Those learners who were interested participated in answering the questions, while the rest of the class passively allowed the noise around them to continue while they hid in the background. Once the modelling and questions took place, I witnessed many learners doodling in their books, some didn't even have their books open, some had their heads in their arms, and others were causing mischief by trying to send notes to their friends on the other side of the room. The teacher was satisfied that a handful of learners had answered questions, and therefore believed that her instructions were clear, but when she set the learners off on the first task, she was faced with several questions – 'What are we doing?', 'how do I do this?', and 'what did you say again?'. I could see the frustration on her face as she thought she had been perfectly clear, and she had already told the class what her expectations were. She then had to walk around the room and have the same conversations multiple times as she repeated the instructions again and again. At this point we were 30 minutes into a 45-minute lesson – some learners were 'busy' with the task provided, and the others were off-task and behaviour was starting to peak. It is funny watching how 10-year-olds can literally make a game out of anything – in this lesson, it was who could throw the eraser the furthest. By the time the teacher had got around to all groups and re-explained the activity, we were at the end of the lesson, so a very quick round of questions was asked as a way of 'measuring success' and then the teacher moved on to the next subject. As I was saying earlier, this is an example of the recitation method, and as Hattie (2023) points out, this can trick you into thinking you have taught the lesson successfully, as at least some of your learners seem interested and engaged, and because they are the ones answering your questions, it leaves you with the assurance that they have understood, but this is just an illusion. As Hattie and Yates (2014) show, learners quickly develop the art of 'opting out' of lessons by becoming invisible. By avoiding eye contact and shrinking slightly into their seats, using tactics to make it appear they are working, they become less noticed and as a result spend their time watching teachers doing all the work while they don't have to.

So how do we measure student engagement? When learners find their lessons relevant, they are more likely to be engaged and motivated to drive their learning, which has an impressive effect size of 0.96. However, there are varying degrees of engagement. Amy Berry (2022) created the engagement continuum to show six characteristics of engagement in lessons. Learners can be just as actively engaged as they can be disengaged, with passive behaviour falling in the middle. I have tried to recreate this continuum in Table 4.3 with some examples of the characteristics you might see in your learners.

Obviously, our goal is to get our learners in the driving seats – driving their own learning. One of the best ways to get our learners to this point is through our clarity and providing opportunities to not only participate but also invest as much in the lesson as possible as this has an effect size of 0.62. We know that boredom has an effect size of −0.46 – another

Table 4.3 Engagement continuum

Disengagement		Engagement				
Active		Passive		Active	
Disrupting	Avoiding	Withdrawing	Participating	Investing	Driving
Learners in this column are actively trying to disrupt learning and display problematic behaviour. Usually, they are the ones who constantly call out or try to engage in discussing anything other than what is being taught.	Another active trait of someone seeking to avoid doing work. They might be the ones who regularly ask to visit the bathroom as a way of escaping the classroom.	This behaviour is much more passive, and these children often are the ones going off on tangents, daydreaming in the classroom. You might have to wake them up a few times.	You can still participate in a lesson while still being passive. They might be doing the work you have set and answer the questions you ask (if directed straight at them), but they don't push themselves further.	These learners are being actively involved in the lesson – raising their hands to ask you questions, collaborating well in their groups, and keen to succeed.	These guys are metacognitively supercharged! They are constantly seeking feedback, setting goals, and monitoring their progress.

reason why we need to stop overloading our learners' minds with our incessant teacher talk and get them involved in thinking more actively, rather than listening passively.

As I mentioned earlier, being busy does not necessarily mean they are learning. When you get students doing more, and you talking less, you can adopt the technique of 'periscoping'. As Feely and Karlin (2023) mention, periscope is a method of scanning the classroom to see what is happening so that intervention can occur quickly, and also making sure the learners are aware that they are being seen and are being held accountable for their actions – think about the good old saying "eyes in the back of my head". They suggest that to do this successfully, you should:

1. Position yourself somewhere in the room that enables you to see the whole room with minimal head movement.
2. Scan the room by moving your gaze from learner to learner. Do this regularly from the same position so the learners know what you are doing and are expecting it.
3. Exaggerate by occasionally craning your neck or standing on tiptoes, raising an eyebrow, etc. Encourage self-correction through actions rather than words.
4. Correct any issues by moving from your position to the learner most in need of your intervention.

Make sure you avoid blind spots when you are scanning the room and ensure that you use correction techniques to ensure your learners know there are consequences when they are off-task.

While this will help with the initial overview to check students are on-task, this next challenge is to measure engagement. There has been much research conducted in recent years on evaluating student engagement and active learning. As part of the Department for Education's Ofsted standards (2021), they state that teachers should be able to 'use and evaluate distinctive teaching approaches to engage and support' their learners – but what does that actually mean? As mentioned in the Department for Education's 2019 Early Career Framework, 'Pupils are likely to learn at different rates and to require different levels and types of support from teachers to succeed' so the challenge is providing learning that is going to engage each of your learners based on their individual needs.

So, let's start by defining what exactly student engagement is. Alexander Astin first coined the term 'engagement' in reference to learners, in which he said it was "the amount of physical and psychological energy that the student devotes to the academic experience" (Astin, 1999). George Kuh further expanded on this concept for the National Survey of Student Engagement, in which he argued that is it not just the learner's responsibility alone to be engaged, but "both the time and energy students invest in educationally purposeful activities and the effort institutions devote to using effective educational performance" (2009). Collectively though, the main consensus is that learner engagement is more than just trying to get them to remember and recall knowledge. Engagement is just as much emotional and behavioural as it is academic. Fredricks et al. (2004) discuss three ways to be engaged:

1. Behavioural Engagement – being able to observe the norms around them and participating in activities.
2. Emotional Engagement – referring to the feelings learners might have around activities.
3. Cognitive Engagement – linked to the learner's motivations.

In recent research, McREL has correlated lots of evidence surrounding student engagement, and has come up with its own definition, stating that engagement is 'A condition of emotional, social, and intellectual readiness to learn characterised by curiosity, participation, and the drive to learn more' (Abla & Fraumeni, 2019). The Collaborative for Academic, Social, and Emotional Learning concluded in their research that the emotional connection that learners have in lessons plays a vital role in the success of their outcomes. When learners are engaged, they are motivated to persist with the learning, even when it becomes more challenging. Engagement is linked to academic success, so we must harness the techniques that are going to fully immerse our learners into their learning so that they can achieve academic success and continuous development.

So, what leads to disengagement in the classroom? Some underlying themes that are common in both primary and secondary schools are usually issues such as lack of relevance. Have you ever tried to sit through a YouTube video on a topic you have no interest in? While I love learning about the history of the British Monarchs and what life was like during the Victorian times, I can guarantee my husband and children would not share the same excited interest. My husband shares the same issue that many learners would in the classroom – that particular subject bears no connection to his goals and ideas of interest (Wigfield et al., 1998). Similarly, my younger children, who are 8 and 5, would definitely struggle to see the connection of the French Revolution to their everyday life. If I want to draw them into my love of history, then I must do what my parents did for me, that is, to bring history to life! As I have mentioned before, teacher-talk and traditional teacher-led lecturing do not suit short attention spans, with young children there must be an element of active learning. I still remember being in year 4 and having to create my own mummy and sarcophagus for my history class – one of the most exciting tasks I was ever given in Primary school, which allowed me to take part in participatory learning. I have mentioned it so many times, and I will say it again – children learn through doing!

Another cause for disengagement can be social and emotional factors. It is then no surprise that bullying or lack of social integration significantly impacts engagement. As Hattie points out, schools are often lonesome places for learners, and if there is a lack of a sense of belonging or a lack of a supportive and inclusive classroom climate, children are going to feel much more disconnected from their learning (Finn & Zimmer, 2012). The OECD (2019) adds to this by stating that students who perceive their school climate as being negative are more likely to become disengaged. Hattie (2023) has given bullying an effect size of -0.28, indicating the negative significance it can have on a learner's prospect of being successful. As learners get older, they face many social and emotional challenges which often divert their attention away from their schoolwork (Eccles et al., 1997). This can further be influenced by family and communities. Lack of parental engagement in the primary years could lead to learners being less motivated or interested in school (Hill & Tyson, 2009). This is further enhanced as learners get older and external pressures and responsibilities become increasingly more prevalent.

Over the past decade, I think it is fair to say that engaging learners has become increasingly more difficult. Some of these are connected to the technological distractions and digital media. While IT has many benefits and is definitely useful in the classroom, it does come with its drawbacks. The influx of devices has led to an increased amount of screen time among our learners. A study by Twenge and Campbell (2018) highlighted that excessive use of digital media often leads to lower academic performance and decreased attention spans – the opposite of what we are trying to achieve in the classroom. Couple this with social media, we now also have to combat a rising surge in mental health issues among adolescents, as researched by Kelly, Zilanawala, Booker, and Sacker in 2019. Mental health issues among learners have seen a significant rise in anxiety and depression as they begin to battle with internal identity crises – often brought on because of social media, which leads to further disengagement and absenteeism. We have also seen a rise in stress and burnout as academic pressures and social expectations take their toll, particularly on our teenagers. There has been a notable increase in learners needing help due to stress and constant worry; perhaps this is partly due to the high-stakes testing culture we have created for learners. As I mentioned earlier, teachers are also under a lot of stress, trying to ensure curriculum demands are covered, and their fear surrounding judgements regarding pay being performance-based. This emphasis on standardised testing and performance measurements can often lead to environments that create anxiety for all (Reeve, 2016). As a result of this, as I spoke about before, we fall back into the trap of traditional, teacher-led approaches in the classroom leading to boredom and disengagement – I call this a Catch-22!

Frustratingly, on top of all of this, we are also dealing with the repercussions of the COVID-19 pandemic. This caused significant disruptions to our daily lives, especially trying

Leading the learning 75

to maintain the engagement of learners through remote learning. As a teacher who also had a 4-year-old and 1-year-old at the time, I can honestly say not much learning was taking place over that year. As we shifted online, and faced the anxiety of uncertainty, it resulted in chronic absenteeism; many times I would ask a question into the void, waiting for someone to respond on our Teams call, while staring at my own camera image, looking back at me in despair. It was almost like that old joke – "Hello, is anyone home?"

Ok – it is starting to feel like that uphill battle again. What character could we possibly play to combat all those factors of learner disengagement? Don't lose hope though; there are plenty of strategies that can help combat this in the classroom. While I know it can feel overwhelming and we are under immense pressure as teachers, it doesn't have to be if you start to make learner engagement a priority in your planning.

A few strategies you could start thinking about are given in Table 4.4.

Another way of building in student engagement into lessons is by adopting the Harkness approach. This approach was named after philanthropist Edward Harkess and encourages a learner-centred method of teaching, focusing on discussion-based learning. While this is not by any means a new approach, it was first developed in the 1930s, it does aim to foster understanding, critical thinking, and active participation amongst your learners. Some of the key features of the Harkness approach are given in Table 4.5.

Recent research supports the effectiveness of the Harkness method in promoting learner engagement, independent thinking, and academic achievement. According to research, discussion-based learning methods like Harkness have a positive impact on student motivation

Table 4.4 Engagement strategies

Contextual Learning	Learners need to be able to connect their learning to relevant, real-life situations. When a learner is able to connect in this way, it becomes more meaningful and relatable. I often hear the question 'but when am I ever going to need this information', which is usually the first sign of disengagement. Making it relevant and showing your learners the value behind it will increase intrinsic motivations.
Project-Based Learning	Project-Based Learning (PBL) gets learners learning through doing, by completing projects over an extended period. This allows learners to experience active exploration and problem-solving, giving them opportunities to take ownership of their learning, and encouraging engagement and enthusiasm. This is very prevalent in the International Baccalaureate curriculum, as learners are allowed to present their findings in ways that are more interesting and meaningful to them. The content is still learnt, but the presentation may differ.
Active Learning	Through strategies like project-based and collaboration, active learning engages learners through problem-solving and group work. This approach helps the teacher to facilitate learning as the learners explore, promoting critical thinking and enhancing understanding through 'doing' collectively with their peers.
Gamification	It sounds simple but kids love games! Why give them a boring task to complete when you could turn it into a competition? Opportunities for points, badges, and leadership boards make learning fun. We all have an innate desire to be the best, so this aligns with our natural desire to win!

(Continued)

Table 4.4 (Continued)

Student Choice and Autonomy	Research suggests that providing learners with choices in activities makes them much more motivated and engaged. This allows students to feel more in control over their learning. When learners have opportunities to choose, their sense of ownership and autonomy increases. Giving them opportunities to select topics for projects or choosing how they will demonstrate and present their understanding gives them more of a sense of pride over what they are doing.
Flexible Learning Spaces	Traditional learning environments of sitting in rows have been the same for hundreds of years – but what impact does this have? Other than allowing the teacher to feel like they have more control, it doesn't serve as an engagement fostering learning space. Being more flexible and using the spaces around you can help you accommodate various learning styles. Create stations in the classroom, or better yet – take the learning outside of the classroom. This links nicely to community partnerships, allowing learners to collaborate with organisations in the 'real-world' so that they can broaden their perspectives.
Differentiated Instructions	Instructions are so important to ensure learning is understood by all in the classroom. We have already discussed the idea of chunking information and being wary of attention spans to not create cognitive overload. When planning your lessons, think about how you will address the individual learning preferences and abilities of your learners. I once had a child who wouldn't engage at all until I found out he loved The Legend of Zelda. From then on, the worksheets were slightly differentiated to meet this interest – just to, at least, get him hooked into the lesson.
Positive Relationship	As mentioned in my previous chapters, relationships are the foundations of any successful classroom. When your learners feel respected and valued, they are more likely to participate in the activities provided. Learners must feel like they are in a trusting environment, where mistakes are ok. When they feel supported, this will boost engagement. This links also to ensuring you have practices that create a sense of belonging and acceptance. Diverse perspectives should be openly valued and integrated into the learning experience.
Feedback and Recognition	Positive feedback and recognition show your learners that you recognise their efforts and achievements. If a learner doesn't think you will look at their work, or show any interest in it, they won't bother to do a good job. However, when they know you will provide timely and constructive feedback, they will be more likely to put in the effort. Your feedback will help them to understand their progress and keep them engaged as they continue to learn.
Social-Emotional Learning (SEL)	Often, there is so much learners need to know that is not on the curriculum, so building SEL programmes to focus on developing their social and emotional skills is vital. Skills such as empathy, self-awareness, and relationship-building help learners manage their emotions and interact more positively with their peers around them.
Parental Engagement	I have already highlighted how a lack of parental involvement can seriously hinder a child's learning. Encourage active participation and communication with your parents. I don't mean by getting them to sit down and do homework with their child – we all know parents are busy people. But make them aware and involved in what their child is doing. Share positive communication about what their child has done well in the classroom, and examples of their schoolwork. With parental support, this can reinforce the importance of education and create additional motivation.

Table 4.5 The Harkness approach

Round table discussion	Placing learners on a large circular or oval shaped table or seating area, promoting equality and open dialogue. Rather than directing their responses towards the teacher, learners can engage directly with each other and build the confidence to respond to each other in a conversational manner.
Learner-led discussions	In this scenario, learners are responsible for driving the conversation. The teacher becomes the facilitator, guiding the discussion subtly without dominating it. Often seen during Socratic questioning and debates. This again encourages learners to take ownership of discussions and delve into deeper understanding. The teacher's role in the Harkness approach is crucial.
Active participation	Every learner is expected to contribute to the discussions being had so that they build an understanding of diverse perspectives. This helps to foster a collaborative learning environment as your learners learn from each other and understand that sometimes there can be multiple conclusions to a topic. Regular participation in discussions helps learners build confidence in expressing their ideas and opinions in a supportive environment.
Deep understanding	The Harkness method encourages deep understanding, questioning, and critical thinking. Learners should be prompted to analyse and evaluate information collaboratively and come to their own conclusions.
Development of soft skills	This approach not only enhances the academic learning of the topic at hand but also develops those lifelong skills of communication, empathy, and teamwork. Learners are actively beginning to articulate their thoughts while also listening to their peers. The skills acquired through the Harkness method are valuable in real-world scenarios, where effective communication and teamwork are essential.

and learning outcomes (Botkin, 2017). This approach transforms the traditional classroom dynamic by placing the learners at the centre, developing their academic understanding, while also building those essential life skills. But, like any approach in education, there can be challenges and limitations to implementing the Harkness approach. This method requires a shift in classroom dynamics, teacher-training, and adaption of the curriculum. However, the long-term benefits often outweigh the initial transition difficulties as your classroom begins to foster a holistic, learner-centred learning environment.

So, I go back to the question in the title of this chapter – who is doing all the work? We know why we fall into the trap of talking too much, but we also know there is a lot of recent research that dictates the benefits of learner-led learning compared to the traditional teacher-led approach:

1 Learner-led learning enhances engagement, participation, and motivation, particularly through student autonomy and control over their own learning.
2 Meta-analysis by Freeman et al. (2014) showed that learner-led learning significantly helps to develop critical thinking and problem-solving skills.
3 Hattie and Zierer (2018) have indicated that learner-led environments often lead to learners performing better academically than those in teacher-led ones.

4 Learner-led learning fosters more ownership and responsibility in learners, meaning they are more likely to be involved in their own goal setting and build their ability of self-regulation in monitoring their progress.
5 Learner-led learning often leads to more collaborative work, meaning learners develop their teamwork and communication skills. This also leads to developing other essential lifelong learning skills such as time management and adaptability.

Chapter Summary

- Limit the teacher talk by creating more opportunities for your learners to take control of their learning.
- Avoid losing your learners' attention by being clear and chunking information into manageable parts.
- Don't overload the cognitive load.
- Embed student engagement strategies to promote active participation.

References

Abla, C., & Fraumeni, B. R. (2019). Student engagement: Evidence-based strategies to boost academic and social-emotional results. *McRel International*. https://files.eric.ed.gov/fulltext/ED600576.pdf

Al-Maqbali, F., Ambusaidi, A., Shahat, M., & Alkharusi, H. (2022). 'The effect of teaching science based on mnemonics in reducing the sixth-grade female students' cognitive load according to their imagery style. *The Journal of Positive Psychology, 6*(2), 2069-2084.

Ashman, G. (2023). *A little guide for teachers: Cognitive load theory* [eBook edition]. SAGE Publications.

Astin, A. W. (1999). Student involvement: A developmental theory for higher education. *Journal of College Student Development, 40*(5), 518-529.

Berry, A. (2022). *Reimaging student engagement: From disrupting to driving*. Corwin Press.

Botkin, K. (2017). Use of the Harkness method in the mathematics classroom. https://capstone.extension.harvard.edu/files/capstone/files/harkness_method_capstone_paper_kyle_botkin.pdf

Bounaji, Y. (2023, September 17). Teacher as performer: Using acting skills in the classroom stage. *Morocco Pens: Ideas Worth Sharing*. https://moroccopens.com/teacher-as-performer-using-acting-skills-in-the-classroom-stage/

Cherry, K. (2022). How psychologists define attention. *Verywell Mind*. https://www.verywellmind.com/what-is-attention-2795009#citation-2

Clinton, J. M., & Dawson, G. (2018). Enfranchising the profession through evaluation: A story from Australia. *Teachers and Teaching, 24*(3), 312-327. https://doi.org/10.1080/13540602.2017.1421162

Department for Education (2019, January). *Early career framework*. https://assets.publishing.service.gov.uk/media/60795936d3bf7f400b462d74/Early-Career_Framework_April_2021.pdf

Department for Education (2021). *Teachers' standards*. Ofsted. https://assets.publishing.service.gov.uk/media/61b73d6c8fa8f50384489c9a/Teachers__Standards_Dec_2021.pdf

Eccles, J. S., Early, D., Frasier, K., Belansky, E., & McCarthy, K. (1997). The relation of connection, regulation, and support for autonomy to adolescents' functioning. *Journal of Adolescent Research, 12*(2), 263-286. https://doi.org/10.1177/0743554897122007

Feely, M., & Karlin, B. (2023). *The teaching and learning playbook*. Routledge.

Finn, J. D., & Zimmer, K. S. (2012). Student engagement: What is it? Why does it matter. In S. L. Christenson, A. L. Reschly, & C. Wylie (Eds.), *Handbook of research on student engagement* (pp. 97-131). Springer.

Fredricks, J. A., Blumenfeld, P. C., & Paris, A. H. (2004). School engagement: Potential of the concept, state of the evidence. *Review of Educational Research, 74*(1), 59-109. https://doi.org/10.3102/00346543074001059

Freeman, S., Eddy, S. L., McDonough, M., Smith, M. K., Okoroafor, N., Jordt, H., & Wenderoth, M. P. (2014). Active learning increases student performance in science, engineering, and mathematics. *Proceedings of the National Academy of Sciences*, *111*(23), 8410-8415.

Gage, N. L. (2009). *A conception of teaching*. Springer.

Governor, D., Hall, J., & Jackson, D. (2012). Teaching and learning science through song: Exploring the experiences of students and teachers. *International Journal of Science Education*, *35*, 1-24. https://doi.org/10.1080/09500693.2012.690542

Hattie, J. (2023). *Visible learning: The sequel*. Taylor & Francis.

Hattie, J., & Yates, G. C. R. (2014). *Visible learning and the science of how we learn*. Taylor & Francis.

Hattie, J., & Zierer, K. (2018). *Visible learning insights*. Routledge.

Hill, N. E., & Tyson, D. F. (2009). Parental involvement in middle school: A meta-analytic assessment of the strategies that promote achievement. *Developmental Psychology*, *45*(3), 740-763. https://doi.org/10.1037/a0015362

Kelly, Y., Zilanawala, A., Booker, C., & Sacker, A. (2019). Social media use and adolescent mental health: Findings from the UK Millennium Cohort Study. *EClinicalMedicine*, *4*(6), 59-68. https://doi.org/10.1016/j.eclinm.2018.12.005

Kuh, G. (2009). The national survey of student engagement: Conceptual and empirical foundations. *New Directions for Institutional Research*, *141*, 5-20. doi: 10.1002/ir.283.

Lovell, O. (2020). *Sweller's cognitive load theory in action*. John Catt Education Ltd.

Milenković, D., Segedinac, M., & Hrin, T. (2014). Increasing high school students' chemistry performance and reducing cognitive load through an instructional strategy based on the interaction of multiple levels of knowledge representation. *Journal of Chemical Education*, *91*, 1409-1416. https://doi.org/10.1021/ed400805p

OECD (2019). *PISA 2018 results (volume III): What school life means for students' lives*. OECD Publishing. https://www.oecd.org/en/publications/pisa-2018-results-volume-iii_acd78851-en.html

Paas, F., Renkl, A., & Sweller, J. (2010). Cognitive load theory and instructional design: Recent developments. *Educational Psychologist*, *38*(1), 1-4. https://doi.org/10.1207/S15326985EP3801_1

Quigley, A. (2018). *Closing the vocabulary gap*. Routledge.

Reeve, J. (2016). A self-determination theory perspective on student engagement. In W. C. Liu, J. C. K. Wang, & R. M. Ryan (Eds.), *Building autonomous learners: Perspectives from research and practice using self-determination theory* (pp. 149-164). Springer.

Reynolds, D. G., & Romano, A. C. (2016). The development of attention systems and working memory in infancy. *Frontiers in Systems Neuroscience*, *10*. https://doi.org/10.3389/fnsys.2016.00015

Scruggs, T., Mastropieri, M., Berkeley, S., & Marshak, L. (2010). Mnemonic strategies: Evidence-based practice. *Intervention in School and Clinic*, *46*(2), 79-86. https://doi.org/10.1177/1053451210374985

Srna, S., Schrift, R. Y., & Zauberman, G. (2018). The illusion of multitasking and its positive effect on performance. *Psychological Science*, *29*(12). https://doi.org/10.1177/0956797618801013

Sweller, J. (1988). Cognitive load during problem solving: Effects on learning. *Cognitive Science*, *12*, 257-285. https://doi.org/10.1207/s15516709cog1202_4

Tauber, R. T., & Mester, C. S. (2007). *Acting lessons for teachers: Using performance skills in the classroom*. Praeger.

Twenge, J. M., & Campbell, W. K. (2018). Associations between screen time and lower psychological well-being among children and adolescents: Evidence from a population-based study. *Preventive Medicine Reports*, *12*, 271-283. https://doi.org/10.1016/j.pmedr.2018.10.003

Wigfield, A., Eccles, J. S., & Rodriguez, D. (1998). The development of children's motivation in school contexts. In A. Iran-Nejad & P. D. Pearson (Eds.), *Review of research in education* (Vol. 23, pp. 73-118). American Educational Research Association.

5 Knowing where to go next

I'm at a crossroads in my life...

As I have already discussed, using a success-criteria is so important, particularly during the backwards planning approach. However, I still observe so many lessons where it is either just something plonked on the lesson slides and never referred to, or not visible at all. Imagine being told you must meet your friend in location B, but you cannot use a map or Satnav to help get you from location A. You might stumble your way there by using your initiative and reading road signs – 50% intuition and 50% luck. But what if you couldn't read at all? You are lost, wandering down roads and highways and before you know it, you're in John O'Groats, Scotland and they are in Lands' End, Cornwall! So, I am going to use this chapter to delve further into the role of the success criteria and the importance of goal setting for your learners.

Hattie discusses success criteria in this newest book (2023), giving it the most recent effect size of 0.88, which immediately tells us that this has an important role in learner achievement. Why wouldn't we pay more attention to it and use it in our lessons? This is followed by an even bigger effect size for goal setting, which is currently 0.90; if that doesn't scream IMPORTANT, then I don't know what does. Both of these elements combined are designed to provide learners with the ability to create clear and achievable targets, having a better understanding of the purpose of the learning, while also enhancing their motivation and focus, by better engaging them in the activities being provided. If I know why I am doing something, I am more likely to do it. You tell me to clean my house; I am going to moan and grumble repeatedly – you tell me family are coming in 30 minutes, and the house looks like a tip, I will have it spotless in 15 minutes with cookies in the oven and a pot of tea ready to go! I have a goal I need to achieve, with a time frame to do it and I turn into a Superwoman. It is the same with our learners, if they know that you are not just teaching them some pointless information they will never need again, they are more likely to see the importance of the topics. Giving them that motivation to strive towards a goal also promotes self-regulation and self-assessment, allowing your learners to monitor their progress and make the adjustments needed moving forward. Remember Amy Berry's Engagement Continuum – this moves your learners towards that 'driving' section.

DOI: 10.4324/9781003482123-5

So, what exactly is a Success Criteria? How do we use it effectively in our lessons? A Success Criteria is a collection of specific and measurable statements that inform your learners of what success looks like in a particular task. Going back to what I was discussing in my previous chapters, it shows the expectations of the end goal. Think of it as the roadmap to get to a final destination, providing the pit stops that you may need to take to successfully reach your endpoint. Imagine driving across the country, but not stopping at the petrol station at all along the way or not using a map to tell you where the next station is. You would run out of gas and probably die of starvation because you can't find the next station to get food. Learners need clear benchmarks where they can stop, reflect, adjust, refine, and continue. According to Almarode et al. (2021), learners should answer these questions:

1 What am I learning?
2 Why am I learning this?
3 How will I know that I have learned it?

Almarode et al. (2021) noticed, from doing some observations, that around 80% of learners could answer the first question – what am I learning? – indicating that the teacher had made the lesson outcome very clear. Following this, around 70% were able to discuss the second question knowing the purpose of the lesson. However, only 30% could point out how they would know if the lesson had been fully learnt. This highlights the fact that these learners were not given clarity of what the steps were to complete the task. When we are clear with what the criterion is, and we take the time in showing the value of it by going through it with our learners, it can have a significant impact on the outcome they produce.

What does a success criteria look like?

I have touched upon this a little bit in my previous chapter, but to delve a little further and provide more examples, I want to come back to those other three questions I want my learners to be able to answer:

1 Where am I?
2 Where am I going?
3 How do I get there?

A success criteria should be able to help my learners answer these questions, because they should have a clear ladder of learning available to them – 'If I am on this step, then I need to do this, this and this to get to this step'. Once you have given your learners the learning objective, then they already know the 'what' of the lesson, but the question is 'how will they learn it?' and 'how will they know they have learnt it?' Almarode et al. (2021) make it very clear that the success criteria is the bridge between the learning intention and the engagement needed to meet those expectations; it defines the learning objective as well as the end goal.

I can't say to you 'this is how you create a success criteria' and give you a formula that works every time. Just like everything, success criteria change depending on the context in which it is being used. If I am teaching a knowledge-based lesson, then I may not have an in-depth success criteria at all. There will be times when the primary goal of the lesson is merely the acquisition of factual information, rather than the application of skills; for example, if the objective is to be able to memorise key historical dates or scientific facts, then the success is simply either you can do it or you can't. Similarly, lower down in a school, during the early stages of exploration, learners are encouraged to engage in open-ended inquiry and creation, so a success criteria might be rather limiting here. For example, if the objective is to foster curiosity and divergent thinking, you wouldn't be expecting specific benchmarks. But I can share the importance of deconstructing what the learning objective is asking and clarifying it through measurable and actionable steps. Almarode et al. (2021) ask that you think about this key question:

What would learners say and do if they have truly mastered the learning intention?

As I have mentioned previously, once you have planned backwards and know what the desired outcome is, and what the students are therefore learning, you will have created a learning objective that is specific and pinpoints what your learners should be achieving. From this, you are able to include observable and measurable actions. What are the differentiated levels of achievement? Think of it like an onion – what is the basic (outer layer) you want your learners to achieve, followed by the proficient and advanced layers? Remember as well, there are many different types of success criteria – some will focus on practices that build to mastery, while some might focus on dispositions and social-emotional learning. Sometimes a success criteria goes beyond the content of the curriculum and are instead the lifelong skills we want our learners to have. In the International Baccalaureate curriculum, they call these Approaches to Learning (ATL) which consist of:

1 Thinking skills
2 Social skills
3 Communication skills
4 Self-management skills
5 Research skills

Other dispositions or characteristics of learning could also be skills such as:

1 Critical thinking
2 Creativity
3 Confidence
4 Responsibility
5 Collaboration
6 Perseverance

Using SOLO Taxonomy and my formula from before – SKILL, CONTENT, SKILL, CONTEXT – here are a few examples of how you can break down the learning objectives to create a clear ladder of success (Tables 5.1–5.4).

Table 5.1 SOLO success criteria for math

SOLO	Success Criteria	Child-Friendly Version
Uni-Structural	**Identify** and state the basic components of the problem.	Find and name the parts of the problem.
Multi-Structural	**Apply** the steps to multiply the fraction by the whole number.	Do the steps to multiply the fraction by the whole number.
Relational	**Simplify** the resulting improper fraction to a mixed number.	Make the fraction simpler.
Extended-Abstract	**Apply** the process to solve real-world problems and **explain** their reasoning.	Use what you learned to solve real-life problems and explain what you did.

Table 5.2 SOLO success criteria for science

SOLO	Success Criteria	Child-Friendly Version
Uni-Structural	**Identify** and name the stages of the water cycle.	Name the steps of the water cycle.
Multi-Structural	**Describe** each stage of the water cycle.	Describe what happens in each step of the water cycle.
Relational	**Explain** how the stages of the water cycle are connected.	Explain how the steps of the water cycle connect to each other.
Extended-Abstract	**Argue** the importance of the water cycle stages and their impact on the environment.	Explain why each step of the water cycle is important.

Table 5.3 SOLO success criteria for English

SOLO	Success Criteria	Child-Friendly Version
Uni-Structural	**Find** one persuasive writing technique.	Name one persuasive writing technique.
Multi-Structural	**Identify** multiple persuasive writing techniques in a text.	Find several persuasive writing tricks in a text.
Relational	**Explain** how persuasive writing techniques work together to make writing convincing.	Explain how the persuasive writing tricks work together.
Extended-Abstract	**Apply** persuasive writing techniques to your own writing and **explain** your choices.	Use persuasive writing tricks in your own writing and explain why you used them.

Table 5.4 SOLO success criteria for English writing

SOLO	Success Criteria	Child-Friendly Version
Uni-Structural	**Select** one language feature in my writing (Adjectives/Simile/Metaphors, etc.).	Choose one writing trick.
Multi-Structural	**Apply** language devices to my writing to create imagery.	Use writing tricks to make pictures with words.
Relational	**Illustrate** effective use of imagery in my work.	Show how the writing tricks make your story better.
Extended-Abstract	**Construct** and communicate effectively and imaginatively, adapting my form, tone, and register.	Write an engaging and creative story using different writing tricks.

Math lesson (topic: Multiplying fractions)

L.O: To **apply** knowledge of **multiplying fractions by whole numbers** in order to **simplify** the resulting fractions.

Child-Friendly Version: **Learn** how to **multiply fractions by whole numbers** and make them **simpler**.

Science lesson (topic: The water cycle)

L.O: To be able to **describe** the **stages of the water cycle** in order to **explain** their **importance**.

Child-Friendly Version: **Learn** about the **steps of the water cycle** and **explain** why **each step is important**.

English Lesson (topic: Persuasive techniques)

L.O: To be able to **identify persuasive writing techniques** in order to **apply** to my **own writing**.

Child-Friendly Version: **Learn** how to spot tricks that **make writing convincing** so you can **use** them in your **own writing**.

English Lesson (topic: Creative writing)

L.O: To be able to **apply language features** in order to **construct** my **own story**.

Child-Friendly Version: **Learn** how to use **different writing** tricks to **create** your **own story**.

English and Gillies (2007) suggest the more specific the success criteria are, the more likely your learners are going to achieve the desired outcome you are looking for (Figure 5.1).

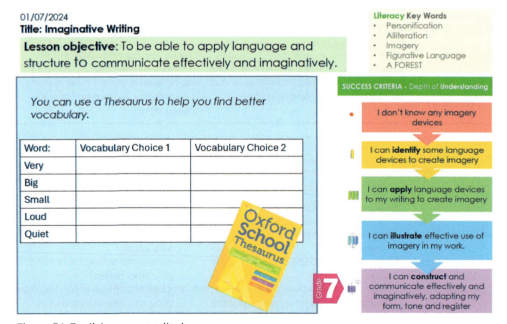

Figure 5.1 English success criteria

Black and Wiliam (2009) also highlight the role that clear success criteria have on formative assessment practices and targeted feedback – when learners can see what parts of the success criteria have been achieved and what still needs developing, they can start to set themselves their own goals.

Why do we need to use a success criteria?

When I think about success criteria, it makes me think about Austen's Butterfly, by Ron Berger. While this is a lesson about effective feedback, I think it also links to the importance of having a clear success criteria as well. Originally, a first grader at ANSER Charter School, in Boise, Idaho had his work documented as he was asked to draw a butterfly. As he continued to get more descriptive and specific feedback, his butterfly drawing transformed significantly between his first and final drafts. This experiment highlights the importance of effective feedback and the power of redrafting. However, what this also highlights is that Austin was not initially given the guidance he needed to be successful initially. At first, Austin was shown a picture of a butterfly and asked to draw it, and as you can see from his first attempt, he created a shape that replicated what he was seeing (Figure 5.2a–f). But as he began to get more feedback, such as colour, shade, and tone, we start to see the butterfly transform. Had he been provided with these expectations and steps from the start, would he have been able to get to the same outcome faster?

Shirley Clarke (2021) discusses some of the questions she is often asked regarding success criteria, one of them being about sharing the success criteria without wasting precious time in the lesson. This is a question I often hear as well, and I do sometimes see teachers spend 10/15 minutes reading through every step of the success criteria to their learners. But what she says in response is linked to what I have discussed regarding modelling examples; if you co-construct your success criteria with your learners, by getting them to compare a 'good' example with a potentially 'weaker' example, the time you are spending on this is being invested as you are providing your learners with the tools to internalise and understand what 'success' looks like. There is no need to 'talk' through the success criteria when you could show them. When you are modelling your example, ask your learners 'What step did I take to get to this outcome?' 'What could I have done to make it better?' 'Is there anything else I need to add to my success criteria?' By co-constructing the success criteria with your learners, they learn about the process not just the endpoint. According to Hattie and Timperley (2007), we can enhance visible learning by creating transparent and co-constructed success criteria with our learners, empowering them to understand the objectives and assess their own progress. By incorporating co-construction of the success criteria into your lessons, you are giving your learners the opportunity to take more autonomy of their learning, which is likely to encourage better engagement (Harris & Brown, 2018).

Often, I hear that success criteria leads to a perceived rigidity, enforcing a prescriptive nature. Many argue that by giving a success criteria, you merely are ensuring all students end up with the same outcome. However, the counterargument to this is that success criteria can actually support creativity and flexibility when provided with an effectively structured framework. You can still provide success criteria without turning your learner's work into clones of each other. Almarode et al. (2021) point out the following

86 *Developing High Impact Teaching*

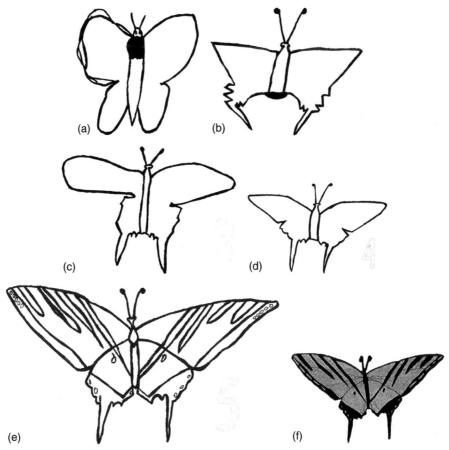

Figure 5.2 (a–f) Austin's butterfly

Student artwork by Austin. 'Austin's Butterfly.' Courtesy of ANSER Charter School in Boise, ID, part of the EL Education network. View online at *Models of Excellence*. https://eleducation.org/resources/austins-butterfly-drafts/

five challenges that often arise when creating and implementing success criteria in the classroom (Table 5.5).

While I discussed the use of 'I can' statements in my previous chapter, a success criteria is more than just this alone. Try not to have a narrow view of your success criteria as you don't want it to become a step-by-step list, nor do you want to fall into the trap of creating circular patterns. The 'I can' statements can still be conceptual and focus on both practice and dispositions. As I have shown throughout this chapter, and previously, success criteria can be conducted in a range of ways from 'I can' to co-constructed breakdowns, use of rubrics, and examples shown through teacher modelling.

What we do need to bear in mind when creating our success criteria is the importance of considering ALL our learners, and ensure we are providing an inclusive environment where all have the opportunity to succeed. Carol Ann Tomlinson's (2012) research on differentiated

Table 5.5 Challenges to success criteria

Circular learning intentions and success criteria	This links back to what I said about some lesson objectives being knowledge-based; the success criteria is a simple matter of can they do it or not? In these types of lessons, there is no deep dive into developing skills – they have either done it or they haven't. For example: *What am I learning?* To be able to multiply fractions. *Why am I learning this?* So that I can multiply fractions. *How will I know that I have learned it?* I will be able to multiply fractions. To try and avoid these circular examples, think about how you are phrasing your learning objectives – what is the bigger picture? How could you include those dispositions in these types of lessons?
Too procedural	Sometimes, when we talk about what makes us successful in school, we focus too much on just doing the steps right, like solving a math problem or naming parts of a plant. This is called procedural learning. But real learning is more than just following steps. It should also include understanding the ideas behind what we do, using what we learn in different situations, thinking creatively, and working well with others. If we only focus on getting the right answer, we miss out on truly understanding and applying what we learn. Try to make your success criteria in a way that focuses on learning that is conceptional allowing your learners to apply their thinking skills.
Product-focused	Learning is like a journey, and there are important steps along the way that help us see how well we are doing. Often, we only focus on the final product, like getting the right answer in math or finishing an essay in English. But it's important to pay attention to the steps that lead to the final product too. For example, in science, instead of just saying 'I can create a model', we should also look at the smaller steps that show we are learning. These steps help learners see how they are progressing and help teachers understand what students know. We should also think about how learners feel and how they use language while learning. Success is not just about the end result; it's about the whole process.
Not measurable	Sometimes, it's hard for learners to understand what they need to do to be successful because the goals are not clear or easy to measure. When success criteria are too vague or abstract, neither teachers nor learners know exactly what success looks like. This makes it difficult to know how to reach those goals. Clear and measurable success criteria help learners practise, think about their learning, and give and receive helpful feedback. If the criteria are not clear, it becomes much harder to achieve these things. For example, saying a learner is successful when they can 'think critically' is very vague – what does that even look like to a learner? How would they measure they had achieved that?
Agenda or set of directions	Sometimes, when we try to make our goals very clear, we end up giving instructions instead of focusing on what we should learn. In math, we might tell learners how to solve a problem step-by-step instead of helping them understand the math ideas. In science, we might give a list of steps for an experiment instead of focusing on what we are trying to learn from it. In reading and writing, we might focus on rules, and in history, we might just list the tasks to be done. This means we focus more on what to do instead of what to learn.

88 Developing High Impact Teaching

Table 5.6 Strategies for differentiated success criteria

Tiered success criteria	Make sure when you are creating your success criteria of deeper learning, your first step of the ladder is accessible to your lower students in your class. This way you adapt your outcomes based on the level of your learners.
Flexible groupings	Use flexible grouping strategies to provide targeted instruction and success criteria based on your learner's current understanding and needs. This might mean you have a tailored success criteria for each group as opposed to one success criteria for the whole class.
Scaffolded support	Alongside the success criteria, provide scaffolding for your learners who need extra support. This could include graphic organisers, sentence starters, or step-by-step instructions.
Visual and manipulative aids	Use visual aids, manipulatives, and technology to make your success criteria more accessible. This could be the use of interactive whiteboard activities, math cubes, or counters.
Student choice and voice	Allow your learners to choose from a range of tasks that meet the success criteria. This can increase engagement and motivation.
Use of technology	Integrate educational technology tools to differentiate your success criteria. Tools like learning management systems can offer personalised pathways for learners.

instruction emphasises the importance of adapting our teaching methods and success criteria to meet the diverse needs of our learners; this includes content, process, and product adjustments. We often talk about differentiation, but this aligns with Vygotsky's concept of the Zone of Proximal Development (ZPD), where learners are more successful when tasks are within their capability range but still hold elements of challenge with appropriate support. Some suggestions for helping you differentiate your success criteria to meet the needs of your learners are given in Table 5.6.

How can we utilise our success criteria to enhance progress further?

So, you have shared the success criteria with your learners, even better if you co-constructed the success criteria with them beforehand – then what? The job is half done at this stage. One trap that I see teachers fall into is not following through with the success criteria and referring back to them throughout the learning process. Don't think of it as a tick box exercise – learning objective shared: done, success criteria shared: done. That is not the end. You need to be encouraging your learners to keep track of their learning so that they build their self-efficacy and ability to self-reflect and adapt where necessary. Having taught project-based topics in Media Studies, I know I have to teach my learners to be reflective and manage their time effectively. They might be given 4 weeks to complete a project, but without a consistent reminder of the success criteria and check-in points, I know my learners will procrastinate for 3 of the weeks, then panic and rush for the last week before the deadline.

In secondary schools, the GCSE and BTEC curriculums often provide the success criteria for you, but I would still talk through it with my learners, as well as modelling what a good

Knowing where to go next 89

Task: Lesson Objective: To explain the learning process and evaluate your magazine.

Research Stage – Week 1:
- Secondary research into other products
- Audience research
- Primary research – what did you do?

Planning Stage – Week 2:
- Mind-mapping
- Planning costumes/props
- Colour scheme
- Finding a name
- Fonts

Editing Stage – Week 3:
- Layering images
- Editing text
- Positioning

Teamwork – Week 4:
- Evaluating how well you worked together/sharing tasks

Success Criteria:	
Pass:	Review the strengths and weaknesses of your magazine.
Merit:	Describe the strengths and weaknesses of the process of making your magazine with detail.
Distinction:	Evaluate the strengths and weaknesses of the process of making your magazine with precise detail and illustrative examples.

Figure 5.3 Project plan

one looks like. Ericsson and Pool (2016) explain how to get better at something by practising on purpose. Here's how to do it:

1 **Set a Goal:** Decide what you want to get better at.
2 **Know What Success Looks Like:** Think about what being good at this looks like.
3 **Find Areas to Improve:** Figure out what you need to work on.
4 **Practise with a Plan:** Do a practice session with a clear plan.
5 **Get Feedback:** Ask someone to tell you how you did.
6 **Think about Your Progress:** After practising, think about how much you improved.
7 **Plan the Next Practice:** Make a plan for your next practice session.

The image above is taken from a Media Studies unit (Figure 5.3), in which my learners had a 4-week window to complete a piece of coursework, evaluating a magazine cover they had previously made. I would start by getting them to think about what the focus should be each week during the 4-week project, allowing them to come up with what they believed they needed to include to hit the 'distinction' criteria (with some guidance from me). I then reminded them of this plan and the success criteria each week to help them monitor how much they were on track. The more we did this, the more I could step back and encourage my learners to self-monitor their progress and keep on top of the tasks they had set themselves each week. While this project is about developing their evaluative skills, it is also teaching dispositions such as time management, self-reflection, and taking responsibility. By giving clear goals, the learners can check their progress throughout the learning, not just as a summative assessment at the end. Having a good success criteria helps learners to know what they need to learn, and continually check that they are on the right track. This is the process of deliberate practice, which encourages learners to grow and become experts. As they grow with confidence, you will see them become more motivated to push themselves to succeed further, driving their learning forward.

You want to ensure you are showing your learners what is expected of them in order to succeed, so to do this you need to make sure you are giving them clear steps right from the start. This means that they can then use the success criteria as a self-assessment tool, where they can evaluate their work against the specific standards that have been set. Your learners can identify what they have done well and what needs improving, encouraging them to reflect and set new goals moving forward. So, for example, if you have asked your learners to write a descriptive piece of writing, and in your success criteria you want them to include figurative language as well as correct grammar and have a clear structure, they can review their work to check if their work meets the criteria and noting areas that they need to improve on. By using success criteria, learners begin to take responsibility for their learning. This independence is crucial for lifelong learning and helps students develop the skills they need to succeed beyond the classroom.

Similarly, this can be used for peer feedback, in which the success criteria give learners a framework for providing constructive criticism. Hattie and Timperley (2007) highlight that clear, differentiated success criteria help provide specific, actionable feedback, which is crucial for learner's growth. Often, I have seen feedback from peers stating things like 'I like your handwriting' or 'it was a lovely story', but neither of these comments is relevant or helpful. You want to encourage constructive criticism that helps create a supportive learning environment where learners feel comfortable giving and receiving feedback to each other. What specifically did their peers do well from the success criteria? What have they not included in their work that is on the criteria? Harris and Brown (2018) further highlight the impact of self-assessment and peer feedback in improving learning (Figure 5.4). The success criteria become an essential guide ensuring that feedback given is meaningful and actionable.

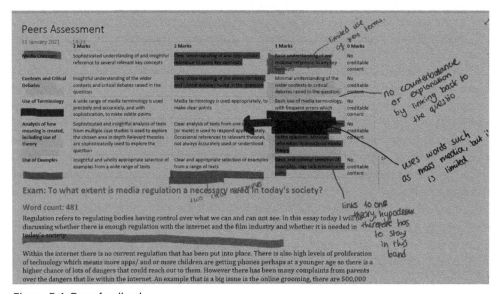

Figure 5.4 Peer-feedback

Knowing where to go next 91

Success Criteria	Confident	Ok	Not Sure
Select one language feature in my writing (Adjectives/Simile/Metaphors, etc).	✓		
I can apply language devices to my writing to create imagery.	✓		
I can illustrate effective use of imagery in my work.		✓	
I can construct and communicate effectively and imaginatively, adapting my form, tone and register.			✓

Next Steps:
To improve I am going to...
WORK ON GETTING THE RIGHT TONE IN MY WRITING. BY BEING MORE SELECTIVE WITH MY VOCABULARY.

Figure 5.5 Self-assessment

Another element to think about in lessons is how you show progress has happened. I will cover more about this in a later chapter, but the key is to be able to show 'this is where you were at the start of the lesson, and this is where you are now'. Using the success criteria in a visual way, where your learners are interacting with their own progress, helps to clearly show them where they are and where they are heading. Using self-assessment strategies helps to reinforce this movement in progress (Figure 5.5).

When learners can see what they need to work on, they can take the steps to becoming more successful – but this also helps you understand where they feel they are so that lessons and activities can be tailored to support the development of these skills.

While we may share our success criteria on our PowerPoints for our learners to see, there are also some fantastic ways of integrating technology to help further support our learners. Hattie's (2009) research on visible learning emphasises the importance of making learning intentions and success criteria clear. Technology can enhance visibility and accessibility of these criteria (Table 5.7).

Table 5.7 Integrating technology

Learning Management Systems (LMS)	Platforms such as Canvas and Blackboard are great tools to use to post success criteria, rubrics, and resources, centralising information for learners, making work easily accessible. These platforms also provide gradebooks and progress tracking features to help monitor learner achievement against your success criteria.
Educational Apps	Apps like Socrative or Formative can be used to create real-time assessments which are aligned with your success criteria. These tools provide immediate feedback, which allows your learners to understand their progress and areas for improvement. You could also use apps such as Nearpod or Pear Deck to help create more engaging and interactive lessons that incorporate success criteria, ensuring learners are engaged and aware of their learning goals throughout the lesson.
Digital Portfolios	Platforms such as Google Sites or Seesaw allow learners to create digital portfolios where they can upload evidence of their learning, reflect on their progress, and receive feedback based on the success criteria. Using these platforms really helps to encourage learners to self-assess and set goals, fostering a habit of reflective practices.
Collaborative Tools	Tools like Google Docs, Microsoft OneNote, Conceptboard, and Padlet enable collaborative work where learners can co-construct success criteria, peer-review each other's work, and provide feedback.
Interactive Whiteboards	Use interactive whiteboards like SMART Boards to display and annotate the success criteria during lessons. This can make abstract criteria more concrete and understandable.

Here you can see an example of where Conceptboard has been used for collaborative peer-assessment, using the success criteria to guide the feedback being given so that learners can see what steps need to be taken in order to improve (Figure 5.6).

So, as I wrap up this chapter, I am just going to recap the key message of developing a strong success criteria:

1 Identify the desired learning outcomes – what you want your learners to achieve by the end of the lesson/unit. From this, create your lesson objective that focuses on the skill you want your learners to use in the context of this particular lesson – **What am I learning?**

2 Break down the steps that are needed to be successful in achieving the desired outcome (think backwards planning!) – **Why am I learning this?**

3 Involve your learners in co-constructing the success criteria to increase their understanding and ownership of the learning process. Spend time discussing the criteria with your learners to ensure they fully understand what is expected.

4 Create a clear and specific success criteria, using a child-friendly language, that can be easily understood by your learners. Make sure they can see the steps that are needed to progress and develop their deep understanding of the task at hand. Make sure the success criteria is measurable – **How will I know that I have learnt this?**

Knowing where to go next 93

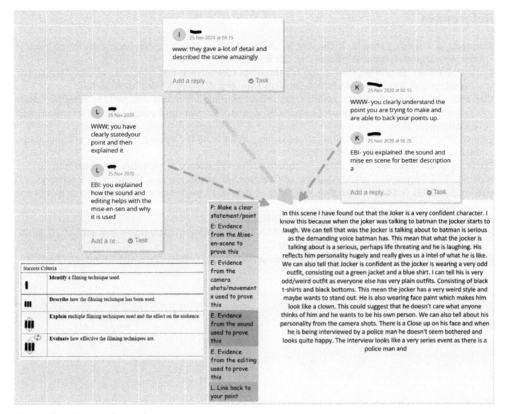

Figure 5.6 Conceptboard

5 Ensure your success criteria is achievable for all by differentiating to accommodate different learning styles and abilities.
6 Keep the success criteria visible so that your learners can easily see and refer back to it. Keep referencing it regularly so that your learners can keep their focus on the desired goals.
7 Use your success criteria for feedback, encouraging learners to both use it for assessing their own work and peer-assessing and providing constructive feedback.

Chapter Summary

- Well-defined success criteria help learners understand what is expected of them so that they can monitor their progress.
- Clear success criteria can boost motivation and focus and promote self-regulation.
- Differentiated success criteria ensure all can succeed in an inclusive environment.
- Success criteria can support meaningful feedback as it becomes actionable and specific.

References

Almarode, J., Fisher, D., Frey, N., & Thunder, K. (2021). *The success criteria playbook: A hands-on guide to making learning visible and measurable*. Corwin Press.

Black, P., & Wiliam, D. (2009). Developing the theory of formative assessment. *Educational Assessment, Evaluation and Accountability*, *21*(1), 5–31. https://doi.org/10.1007/s11092-008-9068-5

Clarke, S. (2021, June 11). What's so important about learning intentions and success criteria? *Corwin Connect*. https://corwin-connect.com/2021/06/whats-so-important-about-learning-intentions-and-success-criteria/

English, R., & Gillies, R. (2007). *Cooperative learning: Integrating theory and practice*. Sage Publications. https://doi.org/10.4135/9781483329598

Ericsson, K. A., & Pool, R. (2016). *Peak: Secrets from the new science of expertise*. Mariner Books.

Harris, L. R., & Brown, G. T. L. (2018). *Using self-assessment to improve student learning*. Routledge.

Hattie, J. (2009). *Visible learning: A synthesis of over 800 meta-analyses relating to achievement*. Routledge.

Hattie, J. (2023). *Visible learning: The sequel*. Taylor & Francis.

Hattie, J., & Timperley, H. (2007). The power of feedback. *Review of Educational Research*, *77*(1), 81–112. https://doi.org/10.3102/003465430298487

Tomlinson, C. A. (2012). *How to differentiate instruction in mixed-ability classrooms* (2nd ed.). Pearson.

6 Metacognition in the classroom – Accelerating progress through effective task design

I have already explained how our brains work, and the strategies to use in order to limit cognitive overload, but now I want to explore metacognition more with you. Cognition is the mental process we go through to know and understand new concepts. Every time we take in new information, our clogs are busy working away creating those schemas and deciphering what is short term, and what will become part of our long-term memory. However, metacognition is the understanding of how learning takes place. In other words, it is our ability to become aware and regulate our own thinking. If you look at the definition of the word 'meta', you will see that it literally means 'beyond' or 'after' – so in this sense, it is what we do after we have acquired knowledge. What do we then do with it?

John H. Flavell is often credited with coining the term 'metacognition' in the late 1970s, in which his research focused on children's cognitive development and their ability to understand their own thought processes. From his research, he was able to distinguish between metacognitive knowledge and metacognitive regulation, in other words, knowledge about cognitive processes and the monitoring and control of these processes. Flavell's work was then further extended by Ann L. Brown, when she began to explore the educational implications of metacognition, and developed the reciprocal teaching method, which uses dialogue between teachers and learners to develop reading comprehension skills through summarising, questioning, clarifying, and predicating.

Metacognitive knowledge is the ability to understand how your brain works, and what strategies to use for learning and problem-solving. We can break this down into the following three categories:

1 **Declarative knowledge** – knowing about your own learning processes and strategies; for example, I know I am a very visual learner, and I am much better at remembering a picture than I am at words.
2 **Procedural knowledge** – this is where you know what specific strategies you can use to perform various cognitive tasks. For example, when I was revising for my History GCSE exam, I would draw pictures to go with specific key dates as a way to memorise important information.
3 **Conditional knowledge** – knowing which strategy best suits the task you are currently performing. When memorising I might use images or mnemonics, but when reading I might skim information before I read in more detail.

DOI: 10.4324/9781003482123-6

When we are thinking about learning, we are conducting metacognitive regulation; this takes planning in order to decide how to approach a task, monitoring and tracking our performance and evaluating the effectiveness of the strategies we have settled on. I always find it so fascinating how our brains work, the level of detail that often goes unnoticed and taken for granted. We do so much on auto mode that sometimes we forget to actually stop and think 'why' we have done things in a certain way. The number of times I have said to my daughter, 'why did you do that?' (usually relating to her annoying her brother in some way or other) and her response is always 'I don't know' with a shrug of her shoulders. How often do we just do things because we have always done it that way? But when we do stop and actually think about what we are doing, we are able to reflect, adjust, and understand the best approaches to cope with the tasks at hand. Metacognition is so important for effective learning because it teaches us to be more strategic and self-directed. Thinking about James Nottingham's learning pit, it teaches us what to do when we don't know what to do. Research indicates that learners who employ metacognitive strategies are more likely to achieve better academic results. Veenman (2010) emphasises that embedding metacognitive prompts within regular classroom activities can foster your learners' ability to regulate their own learning processes. When we know how to regulate our learning, we grow in confidence as we are more able to adjust to our own preferential needs.

Bringing more awareness to metacognition in the classroom is essential for promoting the autonomy of your learners, instilling into them those lifelong learning skills. What we want is for our learners to be aware of how their brains work and what strategies best work for them to become more effective independent learners. This involves using explicit instruction to teach your learners specific techniques to manage their own learning processes (Table 6.1).

Another way of building metacognitive strategies in the classroom is through modelling and scaffolding. Using the Gradual Release of Responsibility (GRR) model is a fantastic way to create opportunities to promote metacognitive development. During this instructional framework, the goal is to move the responsibility of learning from you to the learners; you may have also heard of this strategy through the phases, 'I do, We do, You do'.

Though not a new concept, the GRR model was first introduced by educational researchers Pearson and Gallagher in 1983; it has since been expanded on by other educators and researchers. Initially, the research behind the framework demonstrated that learners benefitted from this structured approach to transferring responsibility; however, Fisher and Frey (2008) continued to develop this model further and showed how the GRR model can be applied across different subjects and grade levels, providing numerous case studies and classroom examples to show how it enhanced learners' engagement. Hattie (2009) further identified how direct instruction (which is a key component of the GRR model) had a significant positive impact on achievement as it helped learners to master new skills and concepts. By gradually releasing responsibility, teachers can ensure that all learners, including those with diverse needs, are supported.

- **I Do (Modelling):** The teacher demonstrates the task or concept, explaining and thinking aloud to provide clear examples. This is where your 'think aloud' strategy is vital in showing learners exactly how the process works. During this part of the lesson, you are clearly demonstrating tasks and explaining the thinking processes.

Table 6.1 Explicit instruction

Technique	Example	Strategy
Goal Setting	Instead of 'I will read more', set 'I will read one chapter of my history textbook each night'.	**SMART Goals:** Teach learners to set Specific, Measurable, Achievable, Relevant, and Time-bound goals. This will ensure that their targets are not overly ambitious or too vague. When your learners know the importance of goal setting, they can make this a part of their internal strategies that they can use the next time they face a challenging situation. **Modelling:** Show your learners how to set a goal – they might not actually know what this is supposed to look like. Share personal examples or walk through setting a goal with the class. One of the ways we learn is through vicarious experiences; so for them to see how you break down goal setting, and the steps you would take to succeed, you can help build their own self-efficacy in how to effectively set their own goals. **Reflection:** Have learners regularly review and reflect on their goals, assessing progress and adjusting as necessary. It is too easy to set a goal and then not look back over it again. The number of times I have seen goals written at the start of the year in exercise books and then never discussed or used again for the rest of the year – what was the purpose of that? Don't teach your learners that goal setting is a tick box activity; instead, schedule in specific reflection times throughout the year. **Visual Aids:** Use charts or digital tools where learners can log and track their goals.
Self-Questioning	Before reading a text, learners ask themselves, 'What do I already know about this topic?' During reading, they might ask, 'Do I understand this section?' Then at the end of reading, they could ask themselves 'what were the main points I have just read?'	**Question Stems:** Provide learners with question stems to use before, during, and after tasks. For example: - Before: 'What is my goal for this task?' - During: 'Do I understand what I am reading?' - After: 'What did I learn from this task?' **Think-Aloud:** Model the self-questioning process by thinking aloud while completing a task. This teaches your learners the process of self-questioning so that eventually they will be able to internalise these questions when completing their own tasks. **Prompt Cards:** Create cards with specific questions that learners can refer to during activities. **Peer Practice:** Have learners practice self-questioning with partners and discuss their questions and answers.
Checklists	For a writing assignment, a checklist might include items such as 'I have written an introduction', 'I have included three supporting points', and 'I have proofread my work'.	**Create and Customise:** Develop checklists for various tasks and involve learners in creating their own personalised checklists. **Guided Practice:** Use the checklists during class activities, guiding learners through each step. **Independent Use:** Encourage learners to use checklists independently for homework and other tasks. **Review and Reflect:** After completing a task, have learners review their checklist and reflect on any missed steps or areas for improvement.

- **We Do (Guided Practice)**: The teacher and learners work together on the task, with the teacher providing support and scaffolding as needed. Working with your learners through scaffolded support, you can then gradually decrease assistance as learners gain more confidence and competence. You might start with the whole class completing the 'we do' section of the lesson; however, as they get more confident, you might set them straight off with the idea while you work with a small group to continue with guided practice.
- **You Do (Collaborative Learning/Independent Practice)**: Learners practice a task either collaboratively with their peers or independently, applying what they have learnt while the teacher monitors and provides feedback.

As Fisher and Frey (2008) point out, there are parts of the lesson that the teacher takes responsibility for and parts where it becomes the learner's responsibility. During the 'I Do' stage, this is where focused instruction is taking place, where the teacher is explaining the lesson objective and the success criteria, employing 'Think Aloud' strategies to model the learning, or giving direct instructions to the learners. During this time your learners should be listening, taking notes, or discussing with a partner their understanding of what the class is learning. One mistake many teachers make is spending too long on this part of the lesson – we want to give direct clear instructions, but we don't want to be the sage on the stage! Remember, give small chunks of information at a time to ensure our learners are actually maintaining the information and it isn't going in one ear and out the other. Fisher and Frey (2008) say that focused instruction is typically 15 minutes or less.

The guided instruction during the 'We Do' stage is a chance to use questioning to scaffold your learners' understanding. During this phase you might meet with selected groups, providing them with prompts to help with their understanding, without giving them the answers. At this point, your learners are experiencing success but with the support of the teacher. Think of it like taking the stabilisers off their bikes but still holding on as they peddle so that they don't fall off. They are doing the hard work of peddling, but you are their safety net if they start wobbling from side to side. Build up their efficacy so that when the time comes to take your hands away, they are ready to soar without your help in the collaborative and independent stages.

One thing to be careful of though, when doing the GRR model – do not stick to it as a rigid framework that ALL lessons must follow. Teachers can reorder these phrases depending on the needs of the learners, and there is no limit to how often you incorporate the focused instruction of the 'I Do', if your learners need you to. Gradual release is exactly that – gradually releasing your learners as and when they are ready. While at the start of your topic you may need to model to the whole class, you might not need to model to them all again in the next lesson. You must use your professional judgement, release those who are ready, and don't hold them back by waiting for you to model again and again when they already understand it (Figure 6.1). So often I have seen teachers make the mistake of using the phrase 'this is my time, you must now all watch me' – don't make them watch you if they already get it! Just like learning to drive a car, some will get it the first time, some might need a couple of attempts at the test before they get it, and some might take five or six attempts before they finally get it – you wouldn't keep everyone off the road until all had passed their test though, would you.

Metacognition in the classroom 99

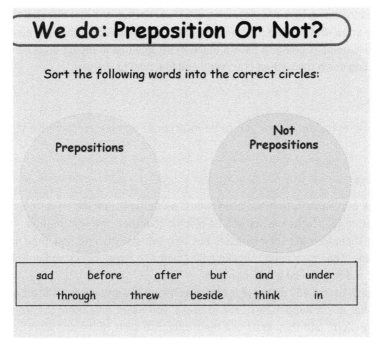

Figure 6.1 We do activity

Again, I want to go back to that age-old phrase 'this is all well and good, but…' – many teachers worry about time! We want to introduce these fantastic strategies, but feel constrained due to time, and being results driven. While, yes, we have an exam to prepare our learners for, or a specific topic that needs covering in a piece of coursework, we must remember that is not really what we are trying to achieve. The ultimate goal for teachers is to be able to create lifelong learners. I want to know that no matter what is thrown towards these children, they will have the tools to think through the problem, find the right strategy to execute, and then reflect on what they have achieved. Metacognitive strategies involve activities that help our learners to understand and control their learning processes so that they can do just that – plan how to approach a task, monitor comprehension and progress, and evaluate the effectiveness of the outcome they have achieved. Schraw, Crippen, and Harley's 2006 study emphasised that metacognitive strategies help learners to develop skills that are essential for lifelong learning. By learning to plan, monitor, and evaluate their own learning, they become better prepared to adapt to new and complex tasks in their future education and careers. By incorporating these skills as early as possible, you can ensure you are putting down the foundations for them to have enhanced problem-solving abilities. The meta-analysis research done on metacognitive strategies has covered diverse educational contexts offering a comprehensive view of its effectiveness. Swanson's research (1990) found that teaching metacognitive strategies had a significant impact on learners with learning disabilities when it came to improving their reading comprehension, and Hattie (2009) gave it an effect size of 0.69. Hattie's (2009) research underscores the substantial effect metacognition has in the classroom so that teachers and educators can rely on this to implement these techniques in their own teaching, fostering a more reflective and self-directed learning environment. We know that putting the time and effort into embedding these strategies into our everyday classrooms is going to have a much more significant impact on learner outcomes than continuing down the path of cramming and teaching to the test.

Activities

Here are some examples of how you could incorporate some metacognitive strategies into your lessons.

Predications

When we ask our learners to make predictions, we are encouraging them to use their prior knowledge from their schemas as well as piecing together new information. The key is to not only get them to make their guesses but also explain why and how they have come to this conclusion. They may need to make adjustments to their understanding following their predication, and this should be encouraged.

In an English lesson, you may give learners an image or a snippet from a text and ask them to predict what might happen next. For example, you might give them the front cover of a book and the blurb, and they must use their inference skills to try and work out what they think might happen, using evidence to back up their reasonings. Or you might ask them to read the opening paragraph of a new story. By asking them to make their predications, they have to read between the lines of the information they have been given and explain how they have reached their conclusions.

Using images, you could create sequencing cards that either tell a story or show the process of something they are learning, which they have to put into what they think is the correct order and explain why they have put it in that order. This is good to use with your EAL learners who struggle with reading.

In science, you might give them a picture of a cell and ask them to predict what happens during a cell division and why. Once they have predicted, you could show them a short animation of cell division and get them to revise their predications – how many got it right? How many needed to make changes to their original predications? This technique could be used at the start of any new topic as a way of getting them to explore the theme first before you give them the answers.

In a history lesson, you could give learners an image from history and get them to predict what happens next. This can be a great hook to a new topic, as you engage them in making their own conclusion.

My prediction is...	I think this because...

Think, pair, share

Think, Pair, Share is a great cooperative learning activity that encourages learners to first think for themselves, before discussing their ideas with their partners and then finally sharing their findings with the whole class. So often we jump in too soon, without letting our learners have the opportunity to really take the time to think for themselves. As Kate Jones points out, 'Don't skimp on the "think"' (2021). We need to make sure we provide enough time for the thinking stage before jumping into the pair and sharing – it is so much easier to just get someone else to do the thinking for us, but we must encourage spending that time in quiet contemplation. I would have a timer on the board, and they had to stay silent for that time. I would also encourage them to write down their initial thoughts (save them just sitting blankly waiting for the time to end). This way you are encouraging retrieval practice strategies as they are required to recall information from previous lessons and are strengthening their own memories. When you don't give them the opportunity to think effectively, they will just rely on their peers to give them the answer instead. Walk around the room as they are doing this, and if you see anyone not writing down their notes, have a quiet word with them; they may need some additional support to get them on the right track, maybe point them in the direction of when you last covered the topic, 'look back in your book to last week's lesson and re-read your notes to help remind you'.

Once the thinking has been done, it is important to encourage good listening skills during the pair stage. Try not to let them all loose and talk all at once – you will always have a dominant person in the pair who does all the talking and the other will not participate. Try labelling the pairs A and B – start with Learner A discussing their ideas first, then give Learner B the opportunity. This way they both get their chance at discussing and comparing ideas. As Jones points out, 'Teachers should actively support student listening, as it's often an underrated element of Think-Pair-Share' (2021). Allowing your learners to pair together first before sharing with the whole class gives them an opportunity to see if their ideas align with each other, and often opens opportunities to further enhance their ideas as they listen to one another. While this is happening, walk around the classroom again and praise your learners for the conversations they are having as this will build up their confidence to take part in the next stage which is to share with the whole class. I would often say to some of my quieter learners 'wow, I really like that answer, I am going to ask you to share that with the rest of the class in a minute'; that way I can make sure they are included in the class discussion, but also give them the time to prepare themselves too. There is nothing more daunting for your shy learners than to be put on the spot in front of the whole class.

When sharing with the whole class, other than those you have already prewarned, use cold calling to select your learners who are going to feedback to the class. Jones (2021) suggests even using the strategy 'ABC – Add, Build, Challenge' to further deepen your learners' understanding. Once a learner has shared their ideas to the class, you ask if anyone can add to what has just been said, then can another learner build on this further? And finally, does anyone want to try and challenge this idea by giving another perspective?

Questioning

A simple and effective way of building in metacognitive strategies in the classroom is merely asking effective questions that are going to promote critical thinking. Often, I see a teacher ask a question and follow up with a 'good job' or 'excellent' and then move on to the next question. These are simply closed questions that are targeted at surface-level knowledge. How do you know your learner really does 'get it'? How do you know they haven't just made an excellent guess? Or better still, just copied what their neighbour whispered in their ear 20 seconds earlier? Questions are not just for show; they should be carefully planned out and executed in the classroom with precision and purpose. Matt Bromley (2023) highlights ten ways to foster an effective questioning classroom (Table 6.2).

If you have read my previous book, you will have learnt about Socratic questioning in the classroom, but just to give you a quick recap, this technique stems from the Ancient Greek period, where Socrates himself laid the groundwork for the development of critical thinking and dialogue. Socrates believed that through questioning, people could examine their thoughts, explore contradictions, and make deeper conclusions. One of the key techniques

Table 6.2 Effective questioning strategies

Philosophical questioning	Try starting the lesson with an ambiguous question – one that has multiple possible answers. This will require your learners to think deeply, while also listening to different perspectives. These questions will usually begin with interrogative adverbs such as 'why', 'how', and 'what if'?
Challenging assumptions	Try to play devil's advocate with your learners; when they give you an answer, challenge that perspective (even if you think they are correct). Ask questions that force them to think about alternative viewpoints, using phrases like 'what if?' or 'who might disagree with this idea?' or 'is this always correct?'
Probe further	Try not to close questioning too early. Rather than falling into the trap of 'good' or 'well done' and moving on, ask follow-up questions to encourage them to provide evidence for their answers – 'how did you come to that conclusion?', 'where did you find the evidence for that?' This will encourage them to begin to think analytically and always provide proof for their answers.
Encourage analysis	Encourage learners to use words like 'because' and 'however' so that they break down their answers into more specific parts. 'I think this because … however, I understand that some people might think…'.
Promote comparisons	Encourage opportunities for learners to compare and contrast so they can see that there doesn't always have to be one answer. It also teaches them how to identify similarities and differences in concepts. Making connections to other learning is a fantastic way to build on those long-term schemas.
Explore consequences	Encourage your learners to think about potential consequences and effects relating to your questions – 'what if' questions help them to explore cause and effect.
Apply to the real-world	To make learning appeal more to your learners, link your questions to real-life scenarios to which they can relate. Ask them to use their critical thinking skills to solve real-life problems.
Encourage reflection	After each discussion, factor in time to reflect on what your learners have learnt and whether or not their thinking has changed at all from listening to other perspectives.
Incorporate diverse perspectives	Allow learners to explore different perspectives from a range of contexts – cultural, historical, and social.
Collaboration and problem-solving	Allow opportunities for your learners to work together to analyse and solve problems, justifying their decisions as a group.

Socrates used was to ask probing questions to stimulate critical thinking through dialogue. Through this technique, arguments could be examined and broken down, questioning assumptions and implications.

This form of questioning is a fantastic way of encouraging metacognition in the classroom. By incorporating Socratic questioning, you are prompting your learners to be more aware of and regulate their own thinking processes. Firstly, Socratic questioning helps to promote self-reflection by encouraging your learners to reflect on their own thoughts and reasoning; by asking questions like 'why do you think that?' or 'what evidence supports your belief?', you are asking your learners to analyse and articulate what they think and why they think that. By making your learners aware of assumptions, they can begin to examine how they came to specific conclusions, but also become more conscious of their own biases and preconceptions. When we ask questions that probe rationale, reasons, and evidence, we push our learners to critically evaluate the strength and validity of their arguments. This in turn encourages learners to be more deliberate and thoughtful in their reasoning, which is a key aspect of metacognition. Socratic questioning helps learners learn to monitor and regulate their thinking by continuously evaluating their understanding and strategies. By asking questions such as 'how did you reach that conclusion?' or 'what could be an alternative explanation?' help learners to assess the effectiveness of their cognitive strategies and consider making changes and adjustments. By continually challenging your learners to clarify and justify their thoughts, Socratic questioning moves them beyond surface-level understanding, encouraging deeper engagement. This in itself instils the habit of continuous inquiry and self-examination. Every time you incorporate this into your classroom, you are also modelling how to pose thoughtful questions and showing the process of metacognitive inquiry. Some examples of Socratic questions that you could use to help promote metacognition with your learners are given in Table 6.3.

Table 6.3 Socratic questions to promote metacognition

Clarifying Conceptions – encouraging learners to think about their understanding and definition of concepts.	What do you mean by that term? Why do you say that? Could you explain that a bit more? Can you rephrase that? Can you give an example?
Probing Assumptions – making learners aware of and question their own assumptions.	What are you assuming in this situation? Is that always the case? Can you provide evidence for that? What would happen if...? How do you know this?
Exploring Implications – helping learners foresee the broader impact of their ideas and evaluate them.	What are the potential consequences of that thought? How does...affect...? Why is this important?
Questioning Evidence – pushing learners to consider the basis of their knowledge and the quality of their evidence.	How do you know that? What evidence supports your conclusion?
Considering Alternatives – encouraging flexible thinking and the evaluation of multiple perspectives.	Is there another way to look at this? What might someone with a different viewpoint say? What is the counterargument?

In order to integrate Socratic questioning to enhance metacognition, start by planning thoughtful questions that require learners to analyse, evaluate, and reflect on their thinking processes. I always say, when planning your lessons, plan your questions as well. Don't just throw out redundant closed questions. Try to encourage dialogue by facilitating discussions where your learners have the opportunity to articulate and examine their thought processes collectively. Offer constructive feedback that will help your learners to recognise the areas where their thinking is strong and where it could be developed further and incorporate activities such as journaling or think-aloud sessions where your learners can reflect on their learning and thinking processes. When giving feedback, ask your learners reflective questions to prompt metacognitive thinking:

- 'What strategy did you use to solve this problem, and why did you choose it?'
- 'How did you decide what to focus on in your writing?'
- 'What do you think you did well, and what could you improve next time?'

By incorporating these practices, Socratic questioning can significantly enhance learners' metacognitive abilities, helping them to become more effective and independent learners.

KWL charts

I love using these in the classroom – such a simple activity that can be used for starters and plenaries brings your lesson full circle. The KWL charts were created by Donna Ogle in 1986 (again – another oldie by goodie!). The purpose of the KWL charts is to activate prior knowledge about a topic before your learners start gaining new information, set learning goals for learners to articulate what they want to know moving forward, and reflect on learning and what new knowledge has been gained.

Simply use some sugar paper or even the desk and divide it into three columns (Figure 6.2):

K = Know
W = Want to know
L = Learnt

At the start of a new topic, ask your learners to simply fill in the 'K' section with bullet points or notes on what they might already know. This works well with an image or an object that is related to what you might be learning. This will help to pique their interest and prime their thinking by engaging them with the material that will be relevant to the topic. Then use the 'W' as a chance to build in guided discussion amongst your learners. What is it that they would like to know more about? Perhaps it is an image of the Black Death, and they want to know why those people (doctors) are wearing weird costumes. Or maybe it is an old VHS and they want to know how it works? I would have this as a working document – you might not get through it all in one lesson but keep referring back throughout the unit you are covering. Can they begin to answer the questions they posed a few lessons ago? Once the topic is completed, they can then complete the 'L' section – what is it that they have now learnt that they didn't know before?

Metacognition in the classroom 105

Figure 6.2 KWL strategy

Another great technique to use in the classroom that is similar to the KWL charts is the 'See, Think, Wonder' routine (Figure 6.3), which was developed by educators at Project Zero, an educational research group at the Harvard Graduate School of Education. The purpose of it is to promote deeper understanding and foster a culture of thinking in classrooms, as part of the 'Visible Thinking' project. Again, using chart paper or any other collaborative writing resource, learners are first encouraged to 'See' through observation, this could be from an image, artefact, or object, in which they are asked to observe closely and describe what they can see in as much detail as possible. We want to encourage our learners to pay attention to what is in front of them without making inferences at this stage. Following this, they are then asked to 'Think', in which they begin to interpret what they have seen. Again, using those open questions, encourage your learners to think about what they think might be the purpose of the object in front of them. What do they think is going on? What might the story be behind what they see? The final stage is then designed to build in questions and curiosity as

106 Developing High Impact Teaching

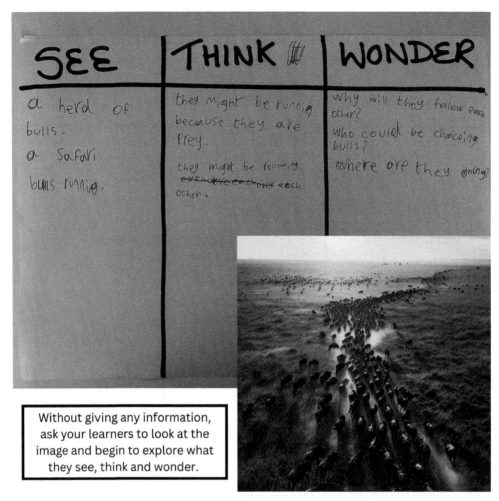

Figure 6.3 See, think, wonder example

they begin to 'Wonder' more about this object or image. What are they curious about? What would they like to know more about? Encourage inquiry through generating questions that can lead to further investigations and learning.

Forming connections

An activity I have always enjoyed using with my learners is taken from Pam Hook's SOLO work on Hexagonal Thinking. The hexagon activity is a fantastic way of getting learners to make connections between concepts, ideas, or topics. This activity involves using hexagon-shaped cards to visually and physically map out connections between different pieces of information. I laminated my copies so that they could be reused multiple times so that students could write on them with board markers and then wipe them clean once they had finished. Each hexagon then represents a different concept, idea, or piece of content, and learners are tasked with arranging the hexagons so that related ideas touch each other.

Metacognition in the classroom 107

Figure 6.4 Hexagonal thinking

Here is an example from one of my A-Level Media classes when my learners were sorting out the connection between Disney and its subsidiaries (Figure 6.4).

I have also used digital versions during lockdown on ConceptBoard, where my learners could work collaboratively online to drag and drop the hexagons into the order they wished to place them. The purpose of hexagonal thinking is to encourage deep thinking and understanding of how concepts are related. Using actual hexagons makes the learning visual and brings the relationships between ideas to life for your learners. Not only that, but it is also a great hands-on activity which ensures your learners are engaged and can collaborate in groups, promoting discussions.

To best use the hexagons in your classroom, begin with making the cards – as I said, I laminated blank copies so that they could be reused multiple times, but you might want to have the concepts already written out on them. Once handed out to your learners, it is their job to link the hexagons together making connections, discussing their thought process and reasoning as they go along. You may want to also ask your learners to compare their connections with the other groups in the classroom and see if there were any different relationships formed. Give some blank ones as well, see if they can add anything new to them.

As Pam Hook points out, this activity has no age limit (Essential Resources, 2022) – this simple activity could be used in early primary school as well as with your GCSE and A-Level leaners. At any age, it promotes higher-order thinking and learners move beyond memorisation into the analysis of information. This activity can be adapted for different subjects and skill levels as it is easily differentiated. It encourages voice and choice as learners have the autonomy to make and justify their connections, and it supports metacognition as learners reflect on their own understanding and thinking processes. By integrating Hexagonal Thinking into your teaching practices, you can help learners develop a deeper understanding and improve their ability to make meaningful connections across different areas of learning.

Feedback

While there are some fantastic activities that can be incorporated to enhance metacognition in the classroom, feedback can significantly improve your learner's self-awareness and ability to regulate their own learning. Start by explicitly teaching your learners what metacognition is and how they can use strategies to improve their learning. Make them aware of the importance of feedback and encourage opportunities for giving and receiving feedback regularly in your lessons. I could write a whole chapter on feedback (in fact I did in my previous book) but I want to just hone in here on feedback that will better support metacognition. When I met with John Hattie, I asked him the question, 'Why have the effect sizes of feedback changed over the years?' – what was once considered to have an effect size of 0.70, feedback is now a 0.58, so what happened? Hattie's response was simple but clear – while feedback became a big buzzword and people started to pay more attention to providing feedback, the problem was that they were not doing it effectively. In other words, everyone jumped on the bandwagon but without really thinking how to best approach feedback. Anyone can give feedback – but what is done with that feedback is the crucial part. Just because you start using your green and pink pens in your learners' book doesn't automatically mean you have given effective feedback. What is the point of providing feedback if it is not being heard? Here are some examples of how you can turn feedback into opportunities for your learners to reflect and use it more effectively in a way that will develop their metacognitive skills (Table 6.4).

Table 6.4 Metacognitive feedback

Self-Assessment	Before giving your learners feedback on their work, ask them to assess themselves first using the success criteria. You might want to use prompts like: • What parts of this assignment do you feel most confident about? • What areas do you think need more work? • What steps did you take to complete this task?
Goal Setting and Monitoring	When you are doing a feedback session, encourage your learners to set themselves specific and measurable goals based on their feedback and reflections. For example: • Your goal for the next assignment is to use at least three different sources to support your arguments. • Let's set a goal to review and revise your work for 15 minutes each day.
Model Metacognitive Strategies	Using 'Think Alouds', model how you provide feedback and show how you analyse the work. I have done this by recording verbal feedback, in which I recorded myself reading an A-Level essay and talking through my thought process as I discuss areas that need improving. You might say things like: • I noticed you used this method to solve the equation. I'm thinking about other methods you might consider and why they might be effective.

(Continued)

Table 6.4 (Continued)

Feedback Logs	Create logs where your learners' can record their feedback and reflections on it with their plans to improve. This way they can keep returning back to it as a reminder of what they need to focus on. This encourages continuous self-monitoring and reflection. When they finish their work, they can look back to their previous feedback and self-assess if they have made those improvements in the new draft. This is great when learners are doing coursework or projects where they are learning the skill of redrafting.
Give Timely and Specific Feedback	As I have mentioned before – give feedback that is specifically linked to the success criteria. Help them understand exactly what they did well and what they need to improve (Green and Pink Pen).
Scaffold Feedback	Slowly increase the complexity of the metacognitive tasks your learners are asked to perform in response to feedback. Start with simpler tasks like identifying their strengths and weaknesses, but move to more complex tasks like creating action plans for improvement.
Use Peer Feedback	Train your learners to give metacognitive feedback to each other. Teach them to ask reflective questions and encourage self-assessment during peer reviews. Such as: • What do you think is the main idea or purpose of this work? • Are there any parts that are confusing or unclear? If so, which ones? • How well is the information organised? Does it flow logically? • Are there any sections that seem out of place or could be rearranged for better coherence? • Are there any arguments or claims that could be supported with more evidence or examples? • How well does the work use examples or evidence to back up its point? • How well does the work meet the goals or success criteria of this assignment?
Rubrics with Metacognitive Components	Design rubrics that include criteria for metacognitive skills, such as planning, monitoring, and evaluating their work. Use these rubrics during feedback to highlight these aspects (Figure 6.5).
Follow-Up Discussions	Once you have provided feedback, have follow-up discussions to check on your learners' progress. Discuss with them how they have applied their feedback to their work and what changes did they make based on their self-reflection.

So, to conclude this chapter, there are many reasons for incorporating more metacognitive strategies into the classroom:

- Metacognitive strategies help learners understand how they learn best and encourage them to make decisions regarding what approaches they should take when doing tasks and solving problems.
- When learners use metacognition, they develop the ability to plan, monitor, and evaluate their own learning which then leads to better academic results.
- Rather than having passive learners, metacognition encourages them to actively engage in the content. Instead of receiving information, they begin to actively think about how they learn and seek their own ways of improving.
- Learners begin to reflect more on their approaches to the challenges set and begin to adjust their methods in order to handle more complex problems more effectively.

Criteria	Exemplary (4)	Proficient (3)	Basic (2)	Needs Improvement (1)
Self-Reflection	Thoroughly reflects on their learning process and identifies specific strategies that worked and didn't work.	Reflects on their learning process and identifies some strategies that worked or didn't work.	Limited reflection on their learning process; may mention strategies but lacks detail.	Little to no reflection on their learning process; does not identify any strategies.
Goal Setting	Clearly articulates specific, measurable, and realistic goals for improvement, with a detailed action plan.	Articulates goals for improvement, but they may be somewhat general or lack a detailed action plan.	Sets goals that are somewhat unclear or unrealistic, with minimal action planning.	Goals are vague or unrealistic, with no clear action plan for improvement.
Self-Monitoring	Consistently monitors progress and makes necessary adjustments to strategies and goals.	Monitors progress regularly but may need to adjust strategies or goals occasionally.	Monitors progress sporadically and makes few adjustments to strategies or goals.	Rarely monitors progress and does not adjust strategies or goals.
Self-Evaluation	Provides a comprehensive evaluation of their work, identifying strengths and areas for improvement with specific examples.	Evaluates their work with some identification of strengths and areas for improvement, but lacks specific examples.	Provides a basic evaluation of their work with general comments on strengths and areas for improvement.	Limited or no evaluation of their work, with vague or no comments on strengths and areas for improvement.
Feedback Incorporation	Effectively incorporates feedback into their work, showing significant improvement and growth.	Incorporates feedback into their work, showing some improvement and growth.	Incorporates feedback to a limited extent, with minimal improvement or growth.	Rarely incorporates feedback, showing little to no improvement or growth.

Figure 6.5 Metacognitive rubric

- With growing metacognitive ability, learners become more self-directed and are able to self-regulate their learning. They begin to rely less on the teacher and become more capable of creating their own learning experiences.
- With positive reinforcement and learners seeing their own successful outcomes, they grow in confidence and motivation.
- By promoting deep understanding and information recall, learners are able to better reflect on their learning processes and strategies, allowing them to better integrate and apply their knowledge, making them lifelong learners.

Chapter Summary

- Empower your learners to become more reflective of their learning through setting goals and self-questioning.
- Incorporate GRR into your lessons to help gradually shift responsibility from you to your learners.
- Provide clear and explicit instruction.
- Encourage reflection and adaptation to foster lifelong learning.

References

Bromley, M. (2023, November 9). A questioning classroom: 38 Socratic questions for your teaching. *SecEd*. https://www.sec-ed.co.uk/content/best-practice/a-questioning-classroom-38-socratic-questions-for-your-teaching/

Essential Resources (2022, February 9). SOLO Taxonomy and Hexagonal Thinking. https://www.essentialresources.co.nz/2022/02/solo-taxonomy-and-hexagonal-thinking/

Fisher, D., & Frey, N. (2008). *Better learning through structured teaching: A framework for the gradual release of responsibility*. ASCD.

Hattie, J. (2009). *Visible learning: A synthesis of over 800 meta-analyses relating to achievement*. Routledge.

Jones, K. (2021, October 13). Getting the "Think-Pair-Share" technique right. *ASCD*. https://ascd.org/blogs/getting-the-think-pair-share-technique-right

Pearson, P. D., & Gallagher, M. C. (1983). The instruction of reading comprehension. *Contemporary Educational Psychology*, 8(3), 317–344. https://doi.org/10.1016/0361-476X(83)90019-X

Schraw, G., Crippen, K. J., & Hartley, K. (2006). Promoting self-regulation in science education: Metacognition as part of a broader perspective on learning. *Research in Science Education*, 36(1-2), 111–139.

Swanson, H. L. (1990). Influence of metacognitive knowledge and aptitude on problem solving. *Journal of Educational Psychology*, 82(2), 306–314. https://doi.org/10.1037/0022-0663.82.2.306

Veenman, M. V. J. (2010). Learning to self-monitor and self-regulate. In R. E. Mayer & P. A. Alexander (Eds), *Handbook of research on learning and instruction*. Routledge. https://doi.org/10.4324/9780203839089

7 Progress in lessons - Know thy impact

Where am I? Where am I going? How do I get there?

While I can give you strategies for improving teaching and learning and we can discuss the pedagogy theory behind how our learners work, really what we want to see is that progress! It doesn't matter what we do in the classroom if there is no progress. Could you imagine running all the way up a hill just to find out at the end we were on the wrong hill to begin with? All that time and effort for nothing! What we really need to be able to do is measure the advancement our learners make in gaining and applying their knowledge, skills, and understanding over time. The goal is to embed those deeper abilities to think critically and solve problems – moving from the surface level into deeper learning, building their ability to analyse, evaluate, and create new ideas based on their knowledge and understanding. Continuous improvement is key to seeing this progress happening, making sure our learners are constantly being challenged to improve, rather than just maintaining their current level of understanding. One of the mistakes I used to make in the early years of teaching was just accepting that 'this child is a C grade child' and doing what I needed to get them that C. Instead, I should have been thinking, how can I push this child to exceed this? Once they had met that grade, I saw that as a job done! I was naive and lacked the understanding that our learners could do so much more if we provided them with the tools. I didn't have the knowledge of how learning works. If a child didn't reach their C grade, I saw that as their problem, not mine. I would reel off the excuses – 'Well, they just don't like school', 'they just didn't try hard enough', 'I did everything I could, but they just couldn't do it'. Looking back now, I realise that actually, I had just as much responsibility as they did. I pitched my lesson to the middle, and if they didn't catch up, then they were not meant to, and those that could have gone further suffered as well from my blasé attitude. What I should have been doing was setting and working towards increasingly complex learning goals, reflecting on their learning journey with them, and identifying areas that needed further development. Progress is about ensuring all learners are consistently moving forward, regardless of where they start, making steps towards being independent learners.

Many educational boards around the world, including Ofsted put significant emphasis on progress in lessons as a key indicator of what is deemed effective teaching and learning. Some of the principles of what many of them see as progress in lessons are given in Table 7.1.

Table 7.1 Principles of progress in lessons

Evidence of Progress	Clear evidence that learners are making progress during a lesson, including how they build on prior knowledge, develop new skills, and deepen their understanding. Are the activities effectively planned to ensure all learners, regardless of their ability, are making progress?
Pupil Progress over Time	Not only in a single lesson but is there progress over time? OFSTED doesn't just look for isolated achievements, but that learners are consistently improving their knowledge, skills, and understanding across a sequence of lessons. What does the data tell us? While learning isn't always linear, there are often ups and downs as learners combat more challenging topics, there should still be upwards movement over time.
Differentiation and Challenge	Differentiation isn't about giving your weaker students an easier task; it is about scaffolding and breaking down tasks so that they can still achieve the same outcome. Regardless of a learner's starting point, they should still be appropriately challenged and supported to ensure they still make progress. Same with your higher end, include tasks that stretch your learner's thinking and promote deeper understanding.
Teacher Assessment and Feedback	How well you are incorporating assessment and feedback is crucial to ensuring progress. OFSTED looks at how well teachers are using their assessments to inform their planning and adjust their teaching. Through continual use of assessment for learning, teachers should be able to adapt the learning to meet the needs of their learners, rather than just ploughing through to cover curriculum content. Hattie (2012) highlights the role of formative assessment in tracking and facilitating progress. He believes that assessment should be an ongoing process that informs teaching and helps learners understand their progress. By providing effective feedback, your learners can understand what they need to do to improve. As I have mentioned before, one of Hattie's most significant findings is the impact of feedback on learner progress. Timely, specific, and actionable feedback helps learners understand where they are, where they are going, and how to get there.
Engagement and Motivation	Remember, it is not about busy work – inspectors like OFSTED are looking to see how well lessons engage and motivate learners. Rather than them just 'doing', they want to see that your learners are being encouraged to have curiosity and are fostering a positive mindset towards their learning.
Impact on Outcome	Where did your learners start, and where do they finish? Relative to their starting points, have they moved on when it comes to outcomes?

Hattie also spends much of his time emphasising the importance of progress in lessons as a critical aspect of effective teaching and learning. He argues that progress must be visible to both the teacher and the learner; the latter should be able to see their own growth in learning, while the former should have a clear understanding of where each learner is in their learning journey. We need to ensure our learners are mastering the material they are learning and moving forward, not just covering the curriculum at a surface level.

Overall, the key focus on progress in lessons is linked to effective teaching. Are your learners making demonstrable, sustained improvements in their learning? It sounds like common sense, right? Ultimately, our job is to produce thoughtful planning, be responsive in our teaching, and make a commitment to meeting the needs of all our learners.

However, there are many misconceptions about progress in lessons, showing a misunderstanding of what true learning growth looks like. Here are a few of those common misconceptions.

High grades = progress

While high grades might show a learner's ability to know and recall content, it doesn't necessarily show a deep understanding of information nor show if the material has moved to long-term retention. If a child starts the year on a GCSE grade 8 and finishes on grade 8, no progress has been made. Great result, for sure, but no progress.

Progress must be linear

Learners will often plateau or even dip in their understanding before they make significant leaps forward. It is important to monitor progress and acknowledge these fluctuations, focusing on long-term growth rather than short-term gains. Cramming for an exam might help you initially get the grade but won't develop any long-term benefits. Effective progress monitoring recognises that setbacks are part of the learning process and focuses on the overall growth trajectory rather than isolated instances.

Covering more content = more progress

Covering more content often leads to superficial understanding and knowledge gaps – the depth of understanding is more important than the quantity of material covered. Remember how the brain works – you need to develop those schemas to create long-term memories and connections. Progress is better measured by how well your learners understand and apply their knowledge than by how much they can cram into their heads.

Progress is the same for all learners

Just like my car driving analogy, don't expect all learners to reach the same milestones at the same time. Learners move at their own pace, and progress may appear very different from one individual to another. Know your learners' starting points, monitor their growth, and personalise their goals. A learner who goes from a GCSE grade 5 to a grade 6 has less progress than a learner who goes from a 2 to a 5. While their attainment is lower, their progress is bigger.

Assessment = progress monitoring

While assessment is a key tool for monitoring progress, it isn't the only method that you can use. Taking a test and realising your learners haven't understood something, but carrying on regardless doesn't help with progress. Similarly, just because a learner has underperformed in a test doesn't always give the full picture. Testing provides us with only a snapshot of our learner's understanding. Progress monitoring should also include observations, learner reflections, formative assessments, and discussions.

Progress is only about academic achievement

Progress is not just about grades; it is also about a learner's social, emotional, and cognitive development. You should monitor the development of their critical thinking, problem-solving, and resilience, to name just a few, to see their overall growth as an individual.

Monitoring progress is only the teacher's responsibility

While we play a very important role in developing our learners, they also are key participants. We should be encouraging more self-assessment, reflection, and goal setting to help our learners take ownership of their own learning journey.

When students are doing, they are making progress

As mentioned before, busy work does not necessarily lead to progress. The activities we give our learners should be challenging, thought-provoking, and aligned with the learning objective. Just being a learner that is 'doing' doesn't mean they are learning.

Being aware of these misconceptions is important because they can have a significant impact on whether or not your learners make the progress you desire.

I want to focus this chapter on some of the key ways in which you can monitor progress both in your lessons and also over time. We should all know the term Assessment for Learning (AfL) and may already know a range of strategies to use in the classroom, this is usually your way of checking understanding in the lesson, and we will cover some more of these in this chapter. But there is also assessment of learning (AoL), using data to monitor progress, as well as assessment as learning (AaL), in which we encourage our learners to assess their own progress as part of their learning journey (Table 7.2).

Let's dive into each of these in more detail and find some good strategies that you can begin using in your classroom today.

Assessment of learning (AoL) - Evaluating the end

Probably the quickest and easiest to explain of the three types of assessment, AoL is simply the process of evaluating learners' knowledge and skills at the end of a topic or unit. This is most typically done through some form of summative assessment, whether that be a test, an exam, or the submission of a final project. The purpose of AoL is to measure how well your learners have met the objectives for that unit, providing a summary of their achievement levels. For these assessments, the focus is primarily on grades or scores and are often compared to established standards or benchmarks to evaluate your learner's progress and attainment in relation to others of the same age. As this is usually completed at the end of a unit, it is often final and, therefore, doesn't necessarily offer opportunities for immediate feedback to improve. While a very useful tool, and necessary in measuring progress and attainment, it cannot be the only type of assessment we use. We must ensure we are embedding both assessment for learning and assessment as learning throughout the learning sequence, to ensure that by the time learners get to the summative stage, they are fully prepared.

Table 7.2 Assessment for, of, and as learning

Assessment of Learning	Assessment for Learning	Assessment as Learning
Final Exams: These are typically given at the end of a course or unit to evaluate how well learners have learned the material. The results are often used for grading and reporting. **Standardised Tests:** Tests like SAT, GCSE, GLs, or MAP are used to measure learners' proficiency in a subject at a specific point in time, often comparing them to a standard or to other learners. **End-of-Unit Projects:** A comprehensive project that learners complete at the end of a unit to demonstrate their understanding of the key concepts.	**Formative Quizzes:** Short quizzes given during a lesson or unit to check learners' understanding. The results help teachers adjust instruction to address any learning gaps. **Classroom Discussions:** Ongoing discussions where the teacher can gauge learners' understanding of the material in real-time and provide immediate feedback. **Exit Tickets:** Learners write down something they learned or a question they still have at the end of a lesson, giving the teacher insight into their understanding and guiding future instruction.	**Self-Assessment:** Learners evaluate their own work against a rubric or set criteria, reflecting on their learning process and identifying areas for improvement. **Peer Assessment:** Learners assess each other's work, providing feedback and learning from the perspectives of their peers. **Learning Journals:** Learners maintain journals where they reflect on their learning experiences, set goals, and monitor their own progress.

Assessment for learning (AfL) – Guiding the journey

AfL focuses on continuous formative assessment throughout the learning process, in contrast to just summative assessments at the end of each topic, helping both teachers and learners in making instructional decisions to support their learning. Mike Gershon (2015) discusses the simple and effective ways to implement assessment for (and as) learning in the classroom, getting an understanding of what learners have learnt and then using that information to inform your teaching. Instead of ploughing through the curriculum, AfL allows teachers to be responsive to what their learners can do and what might need recapping due to misconceptions or misunderstandings.

So many times, I see teachers just sticking rigidly to their lesson plans, feeling the pressure of teaching to the test, or worried they are not going to cover the curriculum if they stop and reflect. It is an old habit that needs to be broken. As I have said time and time again, what is the point in ploughing through, hoping that some of your learners keep up while the rest get further and further behind? When teachers feel the pressure to perform in the summative assessments, they lose focus on what really matters – deeper learning and understanding. The age-old 'we covered this in week 3' doesn't work. Retrieval practice and regular use of AfL will ensure that learners do keep up with the demands of the curriculum, and, even better, they will have a deeper understanding of what is being taught, as opposed to just the surface-level ability to recall on-demand. By eliciting information from your learners as you go allows you to keep on top of what they understand, letting you adapt your planning and making learning time more effective and purposeful. As Kate Jones (2021) points out, one of

Progress in lessons - Know thy impact 117

the misconceptions many teachers have is that formative assessment is only done through questioning; as a result, I see lots of closed questions that often limit opportunities for discussion and development. When eliciting information, you want to ensure you are getting to the root of what, exactly, your learners know. Learners are great guesses! If I ask, 'Give me an example of a prime number', while I may get the response '3' – this could either be a great guess or even just something a mate has just whispered in their ear, how do I know they really understand what prime numbers are? How do I know that they got to that answer using the correct process? Some effective ways of incorporating effective questioning to elicit your learners' understanding are given in Table 7.3.

Table 7.3 Questioning to elicit information

Targeted Questioning	When planning your lesson, also plan which learners you are going to target with your questions and what specifically you will ask. There may be certain learners you want to get information from, perhaps because you fear they might not understand the content of the lesson. By preparing your targeted questions, you will ensure that the correct people are answering your questions.
	This links to Dylan Wiliam's 'no hands up' approach, which encourages cold calling on learners, ensuring that everyone is prepared to participate and engage with the lesson. When you enforce this approach, it limits the number of learners calling out the answer, promotes inclusivity, and keeps all learners alert (William, 2018).
	A great approach is to put names on lollipop sticks and select one at 'random' – this makes it appear to the learners that you don't know whom you are going to ask, but in reality, you have preplanned your questions. Similarly, using different coloured sticks could help you differentiate the types of questions you need to ask different learners.
Open Questions	Open questions allow more chances for your learners to think. As mentioned, closed questions provide short answers that are either right or wrong – which can easily be lucky guesses. Open questions using words such as 'why' and 'how' elicit information based on reasoning. It gives you the opportunity to check, not only for knowledge but also the understanding of the thought processes your learners are taking. 'How did you get to that answer?', 'how do you know you are correct?', 'why is this the only correct answer?'
Bounce Questioning (Redirecting or Looping)	This strategy can be used to encourage classroom discussions to deepen your learners' thinking and peer interaction. It involves you asking a question to one learner, and then 'bouncing' the same or a follow-up question to another learner, asking them to build, challenge, or expand the first answer (Renton, 2020). For example:
	'Student A, what do you think the main theme of the story is?'
	'Student B, do you agree with Student A's answer? Why or why not?'
	'Student C, how would you expand on what Student B said?' or 'Can anyone challenge or add to that?'
	Another technique you could use is Kate Jones' (2021) 'Explanation, Illustration, Elaboration' – in which learners are encouraged to go beyond just answering a question in the simplest form and further extending it.

(Continued)

Table 7.3 (Continued)

Multiple Choice Questions	This is a great example of 'low stakes' quizzing in the classroom, giving learners the opportunity to pick from either the correct answer or the 'distractors'. Keep these quizzes clear and specific, avoiding answers like 'all of the above' or 'none of the above'. The key is to also allow time for feedback and reflection. Dylan Wiliam has pointed out that the best person to check these answers is the person who took the test to begin with. I have often seen multiple choice questions being used on Kahoot – I absolutely love this digital platform. But what I do notice is that many teachers rush through to the next question without pausing to discuss misconceptions. When you see that 5 learners in your class clicked on the wrong answer, this is a teachable moment to then discuss how and why they got it wrong.
Statements	As an alternative to asking questions, try making statements instead. These can be used to encourage class discussions and get learners to think about opposing ideas.

There are many other ways that you can elicit information from your learners as well. Start with how you move around the classroom, circulating and talking with your learners. By circulating around the classroom as they work, you can have one-on-one conversations with your learners, trying to talk to them individually as you go. By doing this technique, you can see them in action and spot those that might need more directing – you may find that you are having the same conversation with multiple learners, in which case you might want to pause the learning, gain back the focus of the classroom, and address the common misconception before allowing them to continue. Alternatively, you could also circulate without talking to your learners; this way, you can listen, observe, and read the work they are producing. This will allow you to see who is engaged in the task, what their body language is like, and which learners you may wish to recap in the next lesson. While circulating, I always encourage 'live marking' in which the teachers constantly have their marking pens available to provide live and in-the-moment feedback to learners, rather than waiting until the end of the lesson.

Another useful AfL technique is the use of mini whiteboards. These can be used both effectively and poorly in the classroom. Again, I have seen teachers get students to write their answers on the whiteboard, hold them up, then … nothing! No follow-up, no checking for understanding; what was the point of it? Kate Jones (2021) highlights some tips for making the most of the mini whiteboards in your lessons (Table 7.4).

One AfL approach I regularly see, which I am very sceptical about, is the 'thumbs up, thumbs down' approach, where learners are asked to give a quick visual signal to show if they have understood a topic. One of the main criticisms of this approach is that it is very superficial as you are relying on your learner's judgement of whether or not they understood. They may think they have understood, and confidently given you a thumbs up, but actually they are so far off what you are trying to teach them. Similarly, putting your thumb down doesn't pinpoint what exactly you don't understand. The approach isn't a bad approach, provided there is a follow-up to it. Again, just like with closed questions – if you don't follow up with a discussion, then what is the point? There is also the issue of social pressure and peer

Table 7.4 Use of mini whiteboards

Behaviour	Reinforce the rules surrounding the use of the mini whiteboard – what are the consequences for silly behaviour? What are your expectations? Otherwise, you are likely to get lots of scribbles and stickmen!
Questioning and keeping it short	Make sure the questions you are asking your learners to answer on the mini whiteboards are clear, specific, and appropriately challenging. How do you wish your learners to present their answers? Whiteboards are pretty small, so it will be difficult for them to write lots of sentences. It is also very difficult to scan over the learners' answers if they have lots of writing on them.
Timing	Think about how long you are giving learners to write their answers. If they are going to need a bit longer to provide an extended answer, then is the mini whiteboard the right tool to use?
Show Me	To avoid one learner holding up the answer and everyone else copying, have a 'show me' policy in which learners do not show their whiteboards until everyone is ready to do it at the same time.
Discuss	There is no point in using the whiteboards if you are not going to then discuss the answers afterwards. Address any incorrect answers without targeting specific learners by asking those who got it correct to talk through the process they made to get there. This is a great way of eliciting those who have not quite understood the work and who might need more support.

influence at hand as well. Your learners may feel pressured to give a thumbs up because they don't want to seem foolish in front of their classmates; the fear of embarrassment may prevent your learners from being honest with their thumbs down. While this technique can be a useful, informal check for understanding, it has significant limitations. If you are going to use this method, combine it with more robust strategies – such as cold calling, bounce questioning, written reflections, or small group discussions – to gain a clearer and deeper understanding of student learning. Instead of using the 'thumbs up, thumbs down', I like to use traffic lights, where I ask learners to use them while they are working. Having traffic light cards on the table, they can indicate to me where they are at while I am circulating the classroom – I know then who I need to go and see first (Figure 7.1).

Another way of incorporating hand signals as part of AfL could be linked to the SOLO Taxonomy symbols based on the success criteria (Figure 7.2).

Each hand signal aligns with the five stages of SOLO Taxonomy and can be used by learners to self-regulate where they are in their learning. However, again, there needs to be training on these so learners fully understand the stages of SOLO and, again, there needs to be follow-up questions and discussions to determine why they have placed themselves into that category.

Another strategy to elicit information from groups of learners is the use of 'Envoys'. This is when you divide the class into groups and give each group a different part of the topic to

120   *Developing High Impact Teaching*

Figure 7.1 Traffic light signals

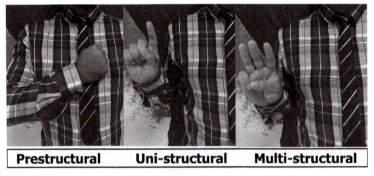

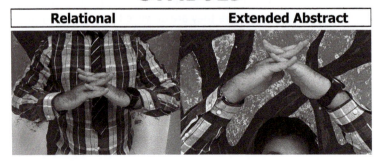

Figure 7.2 SOLO Taxonomy symbols

Source: Chowdhary (2023).

Table 7.5 Envoy groups

Group 1:	Group 2:
Find out as much as you can about the setting in *Of Mice and Men*	Find out as much as you can about the characters in *Of Mice and Men*
Group 3:	**Group 4:**
Research the historical context of 1930s America	Find out about the key themes in *Of Mice and Men* and how they link to the characters

work on; for example, a hook lesson given in Table 7.5 for the English Literature topic on the novel *Of Mice and Men* before they start reading.

After giving your learners enough time to conduct their research and ensuring all in the group were engaged and actively participating, one member of each group is picked to be the envoy, and their job is to work their way around the other groups teaching each one of them about their part of the topic. For example, one person from group 1 goes to group 2 and tells them all they have learnt about the setting and then moves on to group 3 and then group 4. Through circulating and listening to the discussions, you will be able to elicit which group thoroughly did their research, because the envoy will only be able to discuss as much as the group managed to find out. I have also used this technique when wanting to cover more curriculum quickly; for example, with my top set English Literature learners, I would give each group a particular poem to analyse together from the anthology, and then they would go and teach that poem to the other groups so that we got through four poems collectively rather than one as a whole class. Again, this needs careful planning and circulation to ensure you are supporting the learners in both the analysis stage and the sharing stage.

One technique I love to use when eliciting information is the use of Post-It® notes. As a plenary to your lesson, you might put a question or statement on the board and then ask your learners to write their name and the answer on the Post-It® note. You can take the notes in at the end and easily see who was able to answer it correctly, and who might need more support again next lessons. This can then inform your planning moving forward. This works as a form of an Exit Pass and allows you to monitor if there are any misconceptions that need addressing next lesson.

Another way I like to use Post-It® notes in a plenary is to get your learners to write their names and then come and stick it on the success criteria to show what they were able to achieve. If you get them to do it at the start of the lesson and then get them to check again at the end, you can see progress as your learners move their Post-It® notes up the success criteria ladder.

Another technique I like to use with my older learners is a Revision Ladder (Figures 7.3 and 7.4). This is a great way of assessing their understanding of a topic and exploring how far they can dive through the skills. I usually use this as a revision tool, but you could also use it as a mini plenary for your learners or an extension challenge, allowing them a bit of choice. The revision ladder has the six steps of Bloom's Taxonomy from Remember to Create. Next to each step, you give them a generalised task for them to complete; I usually have a bank of tasks for each step so that my learners can choose which one they want to

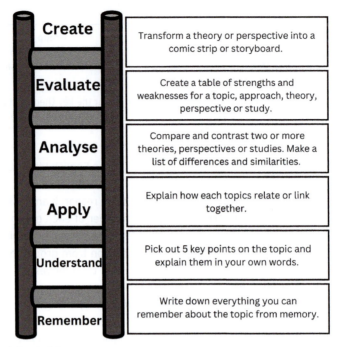

Figure 7.3 Revision ladders

Figure 7.4 Revision ladders

complete. They then work through the tasks, building on each step by applying a different skill.

This is another learner-centred opportunity to conduct a formative assessment as it encourages reflection on learning while also letting you, the teacher, see the connections they are making and where they might need to be challenged more.

Another AfL strategy that I like to use is based on Dr Spencer Kagan's 'Think, Pair, Share' – an effective tool which encourages collaboration, engagement, and interaction in the classroom. For this strategy, you might pose a question or a statement to your learners and then give them some thinking time to formulate their answers, followed by time to pair up with their peers and discuss their answers together before sharing them with the whole class. This is a useful AfL strategy as you can observe and circulate during the discussion part of the activity, hear their responses, and then select whom you would like to share back with the class.

Assessment as learning (AaL) – Empowering learners

While AfL is done continuously throughout the lesson as a way to elicit information from learners and monitor their understanding and often any misconceptions, AaL is the strategy used where learners play more of an active role in their own assessments. When implementing AaL into lessons, you allow your learners to reflect on their learning, identify their strengths and weaknesses, and take ownership of their own progress. Mike Greshon refers to these techniques as:

1. Give your learners the tools to understand how to be successful and encourage them to use this success criterion. As I have mentioned previously, the purpose of success criteria is to help learners identify their own strengths and development needs so that they can formulate their own targets and take ownership of their own learning.
2. Give clear feedback to your learners to show what they have done well and how they can move forward to improve.

AaL will ultimately promote learner autonomy and help embed lifelong learning by fostering a deeper understanding of both the content of the lesson and the processes. This goes back to what I was discussing in my previous chapter about the importance of metacognition. The questions you really want your learners to be considered when assessing their own learning are:

1. Why am I learning this?
2. What do I already know about this unit?
3. What strategies can I implement to help me learn this?
4. Do I fully understand what is being taught?
5. What is the success criteria to help me improve my work?
6. Have I been successful in achieving my targets?

While I have already discussed in my previous chapter the importance of self-regulation in developing metacognitive ability, I won't repeat myself here, but what I will do is give you some examples of how AaL can be implemented into your lessons to ensure learners are constantly thinking about and evaluating their own learning. By providing your learners with a classroom culture that supports AaL, you will ensure they develop those fundamental skills of knowing what to do when they don't know what to do. As James Nottingham (2017) points out:

> The pit is where we struggle to make sense of things. It's the struggle that forces us to think, to reflect, and ultimately, to learn. Getting out of the pit involves using strategies and perseverance to overcome the challenges.

Explicitly showing learners how to assess their own work and that of their peers helps to promote understanding regarding their learning, allowing them to think critically about their own work and leading to them becoming more autonomous (Vigors, 2023).

The Four Square Criterion Reflection tool (Figure 7.5) is used to help your learners reflect on what they have learnt by breaking down feedback into four categories. All you need to do is give them some A4 paper and ask them to section it into quarters (either by folding or drawing boxes). Inside each quarter, they will write the headings, strengths, weaknesses, areas for development, and next steps, then using a clear success criterion, they will fill in each square with their reflections on their performance in each area. Encourage them to write down specific examples, as this will help them with their final square, in which they need to use the reflection to set goals and next steps to improve. This reflective approach helps your learners to identify what they've done well and what they need to improve, fostering metacognitive skills and deeper engagement with their learning process. You could even make this a peer-assessment opportunity, in which they fill in the squares for their partners, but then still allow the owner of the work to complete the next steps based on the feedback from their peers.

Hopefully, by now, you are starting to see the importance of success criteria throughout this book, and yet again, another great way of incorporating it into your AaL is through the use of success criteria strips. This works great for all ages as it is a way of encouraging

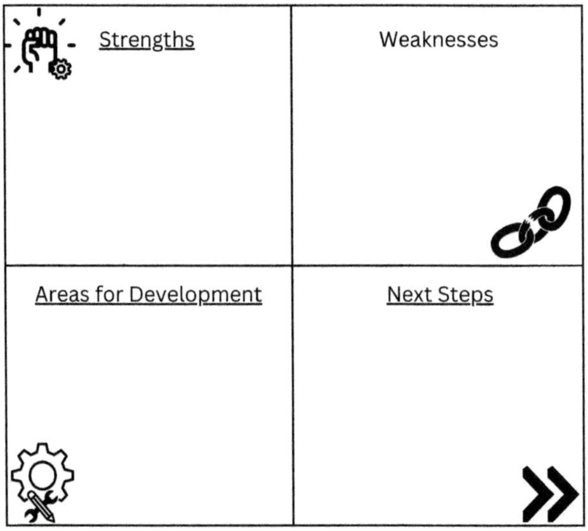

Figure 7.5 Four squared reflection

Progress in lessons - Know thy impact   125

Figure 7.6 Success criteria strip

self-assessment using a rubric. Whether that is a checklist at the higher end or a picture guide for your Primary learners, both reach the same desired outcome of getting learners to measure their success against the criteria (Figure 7.6).

For my old learners studying English, I have given them a step-by-step approach to ensure they are writing strong analytical paragraphs. By giving them a guide like this to stick in their books, they can use it for both peer and self-assessment to determine if they have met all the criteria (Figure 7.7).

Another technique that can be utilised to encourage peer or self-assessment and provide opportunities to give structured feedback is the use of the TAG approach (Figure 7.8). Again, this approach encourages learners to reflect on their learning, identifying areas for improvement and recognising success in their work. The acronym TAG stands for:

1   **T - Tell something you liked**: This first step helps to encourage positive reinforcement by looking first at what has gone well. Identifying the strengths helps to build confidence in your learners.

126 Developing High Impact Teaching

Make a single point about an effect the writer is trying to create – embed a quote
Pick 2 or more words from the quote and **explain** what those words mean.
Analyse why the writer might have used these words. **Relate** it to the historical context.
Evaluate the effect on the reader. How would it make them feel? Could there be an alternative interpretations of the text?

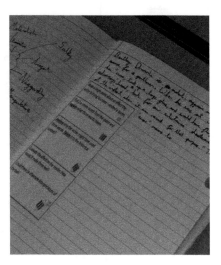

Figure 7.7 SOLO writing criteria

T Tell me something you like	
A Ask me a question	
G Give a suggestion	

Figure 7.8 TAG

2. **A - Ask a question**: This is an opportunity for learners to ask clarifying questions about the work of their peers. By asking a question, it encourages the learners to reflect and think critically.
3. **G - Give a suggestion**: Here is the bit where constructive feedback can be offered with a suggestion for improvement. These should be actionable, allowing the owner of the work to be able to go away and make amendments.

As you can probably see from most of these examples, there is a strong correlation between AfL and AaL. While AfL focuses on gathering evidence of understanding from your learners and using that to guide future lesson planning, AaL begins to shift the responsibility to the learners themselves, where they begin to engage in self-assessment, reflection, and goal setting. However, the integration of both AfL and AaL creates a positive cycle where feedback (from your AfL strategies) informs your learner's self-assessment. As you provide more formative feedback, your learners can then reflect on their progress, set goals, and take ownership of their learning. The synergy between these two types of assessment really lies in their complementary roles in guiding both you and your learners. When these are used together effectively, these strategies not only improve academic achievement but also equip your learners with the skills to manage their own learning for the rest of their lives.

Hattie uses the phrase, 'Know thy Impact' as a key principle in Visible Learning, highlighting the importance for us to have a strong understanding of how our teaching methods can significantly influence our learner's outcomes. When we consistently assess and monitor what we are doing in the classroom, we can ensure our learners reach the desired outcomes we are hoping to achieve. Nothing is a fluke in teaching - all learners have the ability to make progress regardless of how big or small it is. I urge you to ask yourself, 'how do I know my teaching is having a positive impact?' When I went to a presentation by Hattie, he said that if a teacher has been teaching the same way for 10 years, then in reality they have only been teaching for 1 - such a profound statement to make, but so true. Formative assessments allow us to regularly check if our learners are actually learning what is being taught and allow us to reflect and re-evaluate how we should adapt moving forward. Our job is to be the facilitators and activators of learning, and to do that we must use the evidence around us to continuously improve. I am so proud of the journey I have been on as a teacher, I look back to where I was 10 years ago to where I am now, and I know part of that success comes from admitting where I got it wrong, and growing in a way that allowed me to make the changes I needed to make to ensure my learners got the best out of me, just as much as I wanted to get the best out of them. The teaching plateau is a myth - you all have the power to be exceptional teachers, so if nothing else, I hope you take away from this book the importance of knowing your impact and taking the steps to be great.

Chapter Summary

- Don't focus on covering content or achieving high grades - focus on progress.
- Utilise AfL, AoL, and AaL in your teaching to help monitor and support learner progress.
- Be reflective of your teaching to adapt your planning to ensure you have a positive impact on your learners.

References

Chowdhary, C. (2023). *So…what does an outstanding teacher do: A visible learning evidence-based approach*. Routledge.

Gershon, M. (2015). *How to use assessment for learning in the classroom: The complete guide*. Bloomsbury Publishing.

Hattie, J. (2012). *Visible learning for teachers: Maximising impact on learning*. Routledge.

Jones, K. (2021). *Wiliam & Leahy's five formative assessment strategies in action*. John Catt Educational.

Nottingham, J. (2017). *Challenging learning: Theory, effective practice and lesson ideas to create optimal learning in the classroom* (2nd ed.). Routledge.

Renton, M. (2020). *Challenging learning through questioning: Facilitating the process of effective learning*. Corwin.

Vigors, A., (2023, August 13). Strategies to support student self-reflection. *Thinking Pathways*. https://thinkingpathwayz.weebly.com/blog/strategies-to-support-student-self-reflection

Wiliam, D. (2018). *Embedded formative assessment: Strategies for classroom assessment that drive student engagement and learning*. Solution Tree Press.

Index

Note: Page numbers in *italics* refers to Figures, and pages in **bold** refer to Tables

absenteeism 74-75
active 10, 32, 46-**47**, 54, 60, 62, 71-**72**, 73-**77**, 101, 109, 121, 123
adaptive **28**, 42
Almarode, J. 10, 12 50, 56, 81-82, 85, 94
assessment for learning 1, 43, 56, **113**, 115-**116**, 128; AAL 12, 115, 123-124, 127; AFL 12, 43-**44**, 115-116, 118-119, 123, 127; assessment as learning 115-**116**, 123; assessment of learning 115-**116**; AOL 115, 127
attainment 15, 36, 45, 114-115,
attention 8, 14, 19, 24-**26**, 29-30, 37-38, **41**, 55, 58-62, 65, 67, 71, 74, **76**, 78-80, **87**, 105, 108
Austin's Butterfly 85-86
autonomy **28**, **76**-78, 85, 96, 107, 123

Bandura, A. 21, 38
Bandwagon effect 23, 108
behaviour management 7-8, 14, 18, 22, 35, 37-38, 40
Bennett, T. 8, 12, 25, 38
Bloom's Taxonomy 9, 46-**47**, 50, 56, 121

chunking 10, 63, 69, 76, 78
clarity 8-9, 40, 42, 53-**54**, 55-57, 62, 71, 81; clear instructions 8-9, 40-41, 53, 55-56, 98
Clarke, S. 48, 56, 85, 94
closed questions 102, 104, **117**-118; *see also* metacognition
Cognitive Load Theory 10, 62-*64*, 78-79; cognitive overload 63, 66, 68, 76, 95; extraneous 10, 47, 62, 65-66; germane 10, 65; intrinsic 10, 35, 37, 64-67, **75**
cold calling **26**, 101, **117**, 119
collaboration 22, 35, **75**, 82, **102**, 123
complexity 50, **109**
confidence 2, 5, 11, 19, 21-22, 29, 35, **77**, 82, 90, 96, 98, 101, 110, 125
consequences 5, 21, 32, **34**-35, 72, **102-103**, 119
consistency 8, 22, 33, 35, 41
culture 2, 8, 15, 19, 25, 32, 35, 74, 105, 124
critical Thinking 43, **75**, 77, 82, 101-103, 115

deep learning 9, 11-12, 50
differentiation 1, 10, 24, 88, **113**
Dix, P. 8, 12, 15-16, 18-19, 21-22, 25, 27-**28**, 30, 34, 36-38
Dweck, C. 2, 12, 16, 35, 38

Ebbinghaus, H. *61*, 64; *see also* forgetting curve
Education Endowment Foundation 33-34, 38
effect Size 3-8, 10, 15, 22-23, 36, 40, 53, 60, 67, 71, 74, 80, 99, 108
efficacy 2, **4**-5, 11, 17-18, 29, 33, 36, 53, 88, **97**-98
engagement 8-10, 41, 71-81, 85, **88**, 96, 103, **113**, 123-124, 128; disengagement 10, **72-75** 58
environment 8-11, 14-15, 18, 20, 22, 24, 37-38, 58, 62-63, 74, **76-77**, **83**, 86, 90, 93, 100
expectations 3, 5, 7- 8, 14, 17- 22, 25-**26**, **28**-29, 35, 37, 40, 42-**44**, 56, 71, 74, 81, 85, **119**
extended abstract **51**-52; *see also* SOLO Taxonomy

Index

fairness 15, 33, 35, 37, 40
feedback 1-2, **4**, 11-12, **72**, **76**, 85, **87**, 89-90, 92-94, 98, 101, 104, **108**-*110*, **113**, 115-**116**, 118, 123-125, 127
fixed mindset 16-18
forgetting curve *61*, 63; *see also* Ebbinghaus, H.

Gradual Release of Responsibility (GRR) 11, 96, 98, 110
growth mindset 3, 6, *16*, 21, **34**-35, 37
goals 9, 11-12, 42, **72**-73, 85, **87**, 89-90, **92**, 93, **97**, 104, **108**-110, 112, 114, **116**, 124, 127

habits 24-25, 38
harkness 75, **77**-78
Hattie, J. 2-**7**, 10, 13, 15, 19, 22, 36-38, 40, 50, 56, 60, 62, 71, 74, 77, 79-80, 85, 90-91, 94, 96, 99, 108, 111, **113**, 127-128
hexagonal thinking 106-*107*, 108, 111
high-order thinking 1, 50
Hook, P. 50, 57, 106-107; *see also* SOLO Taxonomy

impact 1-6, 8, 10-13, 17, 19, 22, 36, 40, 42-43, 45, 50, **54**, 68, 74-**76**, 81, **83**, 90, 96, 99-100, **103**, 112-**113**, 115, 127-128
independence 11, 90
instruction 1, 4, 8-9, 11, **26**-**28**, 40-**41**, 43, 52-56, 62-66, 71, **76**, 79, **87**-**88**, 94, 96, 98, 110-111, **116**

learner-led 10, **77**-78
learning objectives 9, 11, **44**-*49*, 53, 81-82, **87**-**88**, 115; intention 11, 48, 81-82, **87**, 91, 94
Learning Pit **34**, 96
lifelong learning 11, 78, 90, 96, 99, 110, 123

memory 10, **34**, 55, 62-63, 65-67, 79, 95; schemas 10, 63, 65, 67-68, 95, 100, **102**, 114
metacognition 2, 11, 95-96, 99, **103**-104, 107-109, 111, 123
mnemonics 67-*68*, 78-79, 95
modelling 11, 21-22, **27**, 34-36, **44**, 71, 85-86, 88, 96-**97**, 103
motivation 5, **7**, 10, 13, 24, 33-**34**, 35-37, 50, 73, 75-**76**, 77, 79-80, **88**, 93, 110, **113**
multi-structural **51**-52, **83**; *see also* SOLO Taxonomy

Nottingham, J. **34**, 96, 124, 128; *see also* Learning Pit

OFSTED 15, 36, 38, 45, 57, 73, 78, 112-**113**
open questions 105, **117**
outcomes **7**-8, 10-11, 15, 17, **28**, 43, 45, 50, 58, 66, 73, 77, **88**, 92, 100, 110, **113**, 127

passive 10, 59, 61, 71-**72**, 109
PESTER 47, 67, **70**
planning 2, 6, 8-9, 14-15, **28**, 41-45, 47, **54**, 56, 75-**76**, 80, 92, 96, 104, **109**, **113**-114, 116-**117**, 121, 127
progress 2-5, 8-12, 24, 40-46, 53, 56, 58-59, **72**, **76**, 78, 80, 85, **87**-89, 91-93, 95, **97**, 99, **109**, 112-**116**, 121, 123, 127
Pygmalion effect *17*, 38

questions 6, 9-10, **26**, 30, 42-**44**, 50, 53-54, 59-61, 71-**72**, 81, 85, **97**, 101-106, **109**, 111, 117-**119**, 123, 127; *see also* closed questions; open questions; Socratic

reflection 8, 12, 89, **97**, **102**-103, **108**-110, 114-115, **118**-119, 123-*124*, 127-128
regulation 4, 9-11, 78, 80, 93, 95-96, 111, 123
relational **51**-52, **83**; *see also* SOLO Taxonomy
relationships 15, 19, 22, 32, **34**, 38, **46**, 107
retrieval practice 10, 61-62, 101, 116
routines 6-8, 14-15, 17, 19-29, 32, 37, 40, 62-63

sanctions 32-33
seating plan 22-*23*, 24, 39
self-assessment 11, 53, 80, 90-*91*, 94, **108**-**109**, 115-**116**, 125, 127
Socratic 77, 102-104, 111; *see also* questions
SOLO Taxonomy 9-10, 50-**51**, 52, 56-57, 82-**83**, 106, 111, 119-*120*, *126*
success criteria 1, **4**-5, 8-12, **28**, 42, **44**-45, 48-**51**, 53, 80-94, 98, **108**-**109**, 119, 121, 123-*125*
surface level 42-**43**, 50, 112-113

targets 10, 24, 80, **97**, 123
teacher Talk 9-10, **44**, 59, 61, 68, 72, 78
Think Aloud 96, 98, **108**
Think, Pair, Share 100, 123

Uni-structural **51**, **83**; *see also* SOLO Taxonomy

vicarious experiences 14, 21, 36, 38, **97**; *see also* Bandura, A.; efficacy
visible learning 3, 6, 12-13, 15, 38, 50, 56, 79, 85, 91, 94, 111, 127-128

working memory 10, **34**, 55, 62-63, 65-67, 79; *see also* memory

9781032772653